Expositions and Trade Shows

Expositions and Trade Shows

Deborah Robbe, M.S.

Cecil B. Day School of Hospitality Administration
Georgia State University

John Wiley & Sons, Inc.
New York   Chichester   Weinheim   Brisbane   Singapore   Toronto

The book is printed on acid-free paper. ∞

Copyright © 2000 by John Wiley & Sons, Inc. All rights reserved.

Published simultaneously in Canada.

This publication is designed to provide accurate and authoritative information in regard to the subject matter covered. It is sold with the understanding that the publisher is not engaged in rendering professional services. If professional advice or other expert assistance is required, the services of a competent professional person should be sought.

Library of Congress Cataloging-in-Publication Data

Robbe, Deborah.
    Expositions and trade shows / Deborah Robbe.
        p.   cm.
    ISBN 0-471-15390-7 (cloth : alk. paper)
    1. Trade shows—Management.   I. Title.
T396.R62 1999
659.1'52'068—dc21   99-24970

Printed in the United States of America

10 9 8 7 6 5 4 3 2 1

To the greatest author of all, Christ,
and to my parents, who inspired this book.

ABC Trade Shows
EXHIBITOR

Contents

Preface

This book was written and organized so that the reader could meet and identify all of the major players in the trade show industry, and examine their roles. I wrote the book after six years of teaching undergraduate and graduate-level students—some with little or no experience in the trade show industry. I quickly realized the need for a single source of information that guides the reader through the inner workings of the trade show industry. In fact, most of my students had never attended a trade show!

By examining the components that make up an exposition— exposition managers, exhibitors, venue managers, convention and visitors bureaus, general service contractors, and attendees—the reader will be able to completely design a trade show from start to finish. This will allow you to gain a position in the exposition industry or improve and build on your existing skills. Although each exposition will have different demands and specifications, this book will give you the foundation from which to design and run a successful trade show.

After many years teaching and working in the exposition industry, I am more enthusiastic than ever about it. By bringing in new people and training those already hard at work, we will be able to enhance the effectiveness of our industry.

ABC Trade Shows EXHIBITOR

Acknowledgments

I would like to thank my best friend in the world, my sister, Jane. Bishop Eddie Long, my pastor, continually inspired me to look to Christ for growth, change, and maturity. My faithful dogs, Hercules, Mamie, and Liza kept me company and endured the long nights and days when my attention was focused on the book, not them, and were always happy to see me. Finally, many thanks to my great friends Steven Brown, Lori Ledford, and Chad Caldwell, who lent their focus, support, and words of encouragement.

Professionally, I want to thank the exposition industry experts from the Atlanta area, who have given me invaluable help while I was teaching at Georgia State University. And to the community as a whole, which has embraced the exposition management program and enabled me and my students to learn first-hand all of the inner workings of the industry. Special thanks to the entire staff at the Georgia World Congress Center and Georgia Dome. Most importantly, to Jim "JT" Thompson, who contributed to Chapter 7, General Service Contractors, and encouraged me throughout this project.

Expositions and Trade Shows

**ABC Trade Shows
EXHIBITOR**

CHAPTER **1**

Defining the Exposition Industry

Until recently, the business of expositions was not considered an industry unto itself; rather expositions were regarded as functions of those industries they served to promote or as an adjunct to other industries with which it is inextricably linked—travel, hotel/lodging, and food service. Today, the exposition, or trade show, field is emerging as a viable and separate business category that not only facilitates commerce in all arenas of the economy, but opens new marketplaces at all levels, from manufacturer to wholesale and retail to consumer.

In today's global marketplace, we communicate more than ever through impersonal means, using high-tech electronic systems. Though convenient and effective, these systems lack one important component: human contact. It is human nature to interact; we are, for the most part, collegial creatures. We enjoy getting together to do business, to exchange ideas, to talk things over (see Figure 1.1). And so expositions, trade shows—call them what you will—are here to stay. It is the forming of human relationships that make trade shows work now and in the foreseeable future. Call it the "fiddle factor" if you will, that people still like to touch, see, hear, smell, and taste. Expositions continue to be one of the most effective marketing strategies mix simply because there is no other medium that offers this three-dimensional experience.

The goal of this book is to examine each step in the development of a trade show and to highlight the many aspects of this growing industry.

By the Numbers

There can be no doubt about it: Expositions are Big Business. But though this industry is growing every year, it is still surpassingly misunderstood, even by some of those working in it or closely to it. Most text refers to the trade show or exposition industry as the "sidekick" to the hotel and travel industries, which may be understandable

FIGURE 1.1   Talking things over at a sporting goods trade show.
(Source: Georgia World Congress Center)

considering the economic impact of those economic giants. A study conducted by Deloitte & Touche Consulting Group and released by the Convention Liaison Council (CLC) estimates that $82.8 billion was directly spent in those industries in 1994, a 9.5 percent increase from an estimated $75.6 billion in total direct spending in 1991.

Did You Know?

In spite of the increasing number of "virtual" expositions, improved access to the Internet, and the worldwide link of peoples, markets, and economies by computer, the Center for Exhibition Industry Research estimates the growth of the exposition industry in the year 2001 to be 39.4 percent. Figure 1.2 shows projections of the size of the exhibition industry to 2000.

	1996	2000	Additional Facts:
Exhibitions	4,400	4,781	• Regional off-shoots of established events will generate nearly one half of the new exhibition in the decade ahead.
Attendees	101 million	140 million	
Exhibiting Companies	1.25 million	1.3 million	• Nearly 1/4 of the new shows will be created by taking specialized vertical segments from broad based shows.
Square Feet (used)	448 million	550 million	
Total Exhibit Space (sq. ft.)	63.4 million	70.9 million	• Roughly 11% of the new shows this decade (1991–2000) will be horizontally broad-based shows.
*All figures include Canada and the USA.			• Emerging technologies such as environment technology, biotechnology, and even some currently not developed will spark 21% of new shows in the next 10 years.

FIGURE 1.2 Anticipated growth of the exhibition industry between 1996 and 2000. (Source: © 1999 by *Tradeshow Week*®, Los Angeles, CA (323) 965-5335. Reprinted with permission.)

How much does direct spending in the convention, exposition, meeting and domestic travel industry contribute to the general economy? Considered as a single entity, the convention, exposition, meeting, and incentive travel industry, at $80.7 billion, ranked twenty-second among all U.S. private sector industries, as defined by the U.S. Department of Commerce, in terms of contribution to the 1993 Gross Domestic Product (GDP; the market value of all final goods and services produced in the country within a certain time period.) Real estate, at $718.5 billion, ranked first.

If those numbers don't convince you, consider this: In 1994, direct spending related to conventions and expositions was estimated to be $52.3 billion, or 63.1 percent of the total of $82.8 billion. Association and corporate meetings generated an estimated $27.0 billion, and incentive travel produced an estimated $3.5 billion indirect spending (see Figure 1.3).

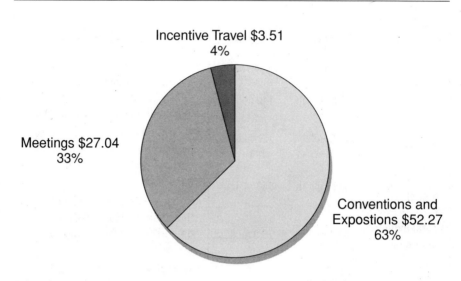

FIGURE 1.3 Total direct spending by industry segment (in billions of dollars). (Source: © 1999 by *Tradeshow Week* ®, Los Angeles, CA (323) 965-5335. Reprinted with permission.)

Hotels and other meeting places received the largest piece of 1994's $82.8 billion total expenditure, $26.9 billion (32.5 percent). They also captured the biggest share of the convention and exposition industry's $52.3 million total: $18.4 million, or 35.2 percent. Air transportation was next both for the industry overall and for conventions and expositions, followed by restaurants.

The exposition industry's impact on the hotel business is substantial when considered from another perspective: Of the hotel industry's $66 billion operating revenue in 1994, the conventions, expositions, meeting and incentive travel industry accounted for $23.8 billion (36.1 percent). Conventions and expositions alone accounted for $16.6 billion (25.2 percent) of the hotel industry's total operating revenue (see Figure 1.4).

In terms of numbers of people, consider that in 1994, an estimated 73.2 million delegates, attendees, exhibitors, other meeting participants and incentive travelers took part in activities related to conventions, expositions, meetings, and incentive travel. Of these, some 57.5 million were out-of-town delegates who traveled to the event, requiring an estimated 143.6 million room nights (based on a 2.5 night average length of stay).

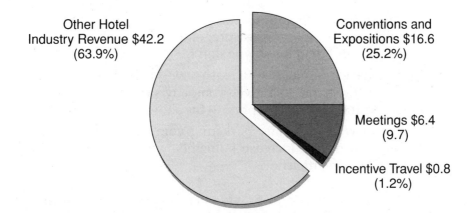

Other Hotel Industry Revenue $42.2 (63.9%)

Conventions and Expositions $16.6 (25.2%)

Meetings $6.4 (9.7)

Incentive Travel $0.8 (1.2%)

FIGURE 1.4 The pie chart shows the financial impact of the exposition industry on the hotel and lodging industry. Spending is shown as a percentage of hotel industry operating revenue in billions of dollars. (Source: Center for Exhibition Industry Research)

Another study, commissioned by the Center for Exhibition Industry Research (CEIR) and conducted by Deloitte & Touche Consulting Group in 1996 gives marketers all the ammunition they need to justify their firms' participation in exhibitions.* Results of the study, titled "Maximizing the Role of Exhibitions in the Total Marketing Mix: The Power of Exhibitions II," concluded:

- Many companies use exhibitions in the selling process more than they do business-to-business advertising, direct mail, or public relations.
- Exhibitions are more effective than advertising, direct mail, and other marketing media components in generating sales leads, introducing new products, and resulting in orders.
- Some 91 percent of business decision makers report that exhibitions are "extremely useful" sources of purchasing information. They rank exhibitions number one for purchasing information among 13 sales and marketing tools.

---

*As reported in *Tradeshow Week*, June 3, 1996, Vol. 26, No. 2.

- Exhibitors who integrate marketing tools in their trade show activities, as well as set, measure, and quantify objectives, are more successful than those who don't.

- Exhibitions help companies to reach new prospective customers. Only 1 in 10 visitors to a given company's exhibit has had any contact with that company prior to the show.

- Exhibitors who integrate marketing components into a total exhibition program increase both their visitor attraction and lead conversion efficiency.

The study also aimed to provide benchmarks and "best practices" to maximize exhibition participation, reporting that exhibitions account for 14 percent of marketing dollars allotted for a product, followed by advertising (11.5 percent; defined in the study as business-to-business print advertising only), direct mail (9 percent), public relations (6.5 percent) and telemarketing (5 percent). Only direct sales ranked higher, at 47 percent, but it must be noted that trade shows contain a strong component of direct/field sales, since sales staffs often invite customers and prospects to shows where the firms are exhibiting.

The study also surveyed respondents as to which of the following marketing components were most effective in achieving their objectives:

1. Generating sales leads.
2. Introducing new products.
3. Taking orders.
4. Promoting brand image/visibility.
5. Promoting company awareness.
6. Entering new markets/regions.

Second to promoting brand image, respondents rated exhibitions as more effective than business-to-business advertising for each component. In reaching objectives, respondents also rated exhibitions highest except for promoting brand image.

The study also examined what successful exhibitors do to attract qualified visitors to their booths and convert them to sales leads. It found that exhibitors who fully integrated the entire marketing mix into their exhibition programs were more successful than those who didn't. Companies that use the entire range of marketing activities—pre- and at-show advertising, targeted direct mail, sponsorships, hospitality, public relations and telemarketing—are more likely to have successful trade show programs. Successful exhibitors see increases in conversions to qualified leads attributable to preshow promotion (50-plus percent), at-show hospitality (62-plus percent) and staff training (68-plus percent).

Importance of Expositions to Other Industries

In addition to the companies that participate in expositions, the trade show industry impacts many others, none more so than what's called the hospitality industry, especially in those cities and countries that depend on income from hospitality-related business. Many hotels are built along "convention corridors," that is, near convention centers or trade show pavilions. The lodging tax alone that hotels charge their guests (who are often attendees of the nearby trade shows) can add up to serious economic power. In most cities, this tax ranges from 3 to 10 percent. For example, in Atlanta, Georgia, the total lodging tax collected for 1998 was $37 million. Of that amount, the Atlanta Convention and Visitors Bureau received $8 million to promote tourism and the convention industry. In larger cities that host numerous conventions and trade shows, the total lodging tax received can run into the millions of dollars, and usually funds the convention and visitor's bureau.

Likewise, the food service industry benefits from the influx of business from conventions. Everyone has to eat, and from exhibitors entertaining their clients to attendees grabbing a quick bite at a fast-food restaurant, the money pours in. It doesn't hurt that most trade show attendees are on expense accounts and will frequently dine in more expensive restaurants than they would if on their own budgets.

Shopping malls and other entertainment attractions of all kinds, too, are benefactors of trade shows. Many exhibitor companies include such "bennies" as golf or tennis outings as part of the enticement to potential clients.

All those numbers are impressive, but they are just numbers, and there's more to the exposition industry than that—much more—and it is the purpose of this book to explain the inner and outer workings of this important business, for it is necessary that its members truly understand it to ensure its continued advancement and long-term survival.

Simply put, if trade shows are not profitable for exhibiting companies they will not continue to participate. It is essential that those working in the exposition industry understand where the profit comes from and how to sustain and enhance that profit.

From Tents to Trade Shows

But before we delve into the "behind-the-scenes" aspects of the trade show world, it may be helpful to learn something of its history; and in the case of the exposition industry, that history is a long one. The word *exposition* today has several meanings, which have changed over time and among areas of specialization, but they all date from the fifteenth-century Latin verb *exponere*, meaning "to set forth, to explain" (*Merriam Webster's Collegiate Dictionary, Tenth Edition*). The definition most appropriate for our purposes is "to show, display, or exhibit products or services for public or private view."

There have always been "trade shows," though certainly they weren't called that. They were regarded as forms of "the market." Indeed, "market day" is still prevalent throughout Europe and elsewhere in the world. The Bible tells of exhibitions staged to show off the wealth of kings. Merchants would bring their wares to display, sell, and barter, while visitors came to socialize and to shop. Trade fairs, the near relatives of trade shows, grew up around religious pilgrimages, whose weary travelers gathered in courtyards near churches or camps. The book of Ezekiel contains a vivid description of such a trade fair. And the book of Esther recounts the story of a king who staged a six-month long festival for his subjects. It's not difficult to imagine the colorful dress of these merchants—the "exhibitors"—and the exotic displays of goods. There was food, jewelry, clothing, and fragrant incense and oils.

Note

In this book, the terms "exposition," "exhibition," and "trade show" are used interchangeably.

In fact, in all recorded history, there are reports of trade caravans throughout the world. Indeed, it was the interest in the trade of goods that propelled much of the travel and the exploration from earliest times. But the modern concept of the exposition, the trade show, in one place, under one "tent," so to speak, is generally agreed to have been set up in Hyde Park, London, England, at the Crystal Palace for the Great Exhibition in 1851. It was in this marvel of architecture, designed by Sir Joseph Paxton, a combination of iron, glass, and wood, where the products of the commonwealth and all her territories were laid out.

Twenty-five years later, the first formal exposition in the United States was held in Philadelphia, Pennsylvania, to celebrate the young nation's centennial. The highlight of the show was Alexander Graham Bell's invention, the telephone.

But for many years, in this country, the exposition of wares continued to be one of movement. Indeed, with the invention of the automobile and the building of the highway system across the United States, the selling goods and services took to the road as never before, giving rise to a new profession: the door-to-door, or traveling, salesman. This form of marketing and promotion boosted revenues and expanded customer reach for many companies and their products.

As effective as this proved to be, traveling sales had their obvious limitations: a single salesman (it was only men in those early days) could visit only a small number of clients in any day; and he couldn't stay long in one place before having to move on. So availability and convenience were not selling points. Before long, it became clear that it would be much more efficient for the clients to come to the salesmen, and the hotel-room display was born. This proved more effective and economical for a number of important reasons:

- It was cheaper for companies to set up products and salesmen in one room for extended periods of time.
- Salesmen could service many more clients in one day.
- No longer restricted by what they could carry in a case, salesmen could offer and display more products, and much more effectively.
- Salesmen no longer had to interrupt their clients' workday; instead, clients came at their convenience. Consequently, they could concentrate on the sales pitch; generally, if they had taken the time to come to see the product, they were ready to buy. (We now call them *qualified buyers*.)

- Competitors could display near one another, enabling clients to comparison shop instead of having one salesman after another disrupt their workday.

It wasn't long before hotel rooms weren't big enough, and salesmen began to rent hotel ballrooms. In due course, they outgrew those, too, and by 1928, companies began working together to find the most effective way to promote and sell their products and services. The National Association of Exhibition Managers was formed, with the mission to construct buildings specifically designed to hold larger sales shows and conventions.

Almost 20 years later, with the end of World War II, the economy boomed and people became more mobile than ever before. Companies began to take advantage of the trade show "centers," inviting clients and potential clients from all over the country to one meeting place. Soon, convention centers sprung up seemingly overnight in cities that had large airports, thus linking the trade shows and the travel industry, and ultimately, the hospitality industry, comprising hotel/motel accommodations, food service, and entertainment.

Show Types

We've come a long way from tents and salespeople servicing their clients out of suitcases. Currently, there are two basic categories of shows: *trade* and *consumer*, either of which can be *vertical* or *horizontal*. There are also *international* and *consolidation* shows. Let's discuss them each in turn.

Did You Know?

There can be no doubt as to the superior effectiveness of trade shows over individual sales calls. Various studies conducted by the Center for Exhibition Industry Research indicates that the average cost of a trade show contact is $162.00 per visitor, while the average cost of a sales call is $277.00. When you add in the average number of calls it usually takes to close a single deal, the figures are $550.00 for trade shows versus $997.00 for sales calls (see Figure 1.5).

	Expositions	Field Sales Call
Cost per contact	$162	$277
No. of follow-up contacts to close a sale	1.4 = $388	2.6 = $720
Net cost to initiate and close sale	$550	$997

The cost of doing business at expositions is almost half (45%) than that of the more traditional direct selling approach.

FIGURE 1.5 The fiscal components of the business of expositions. (Source: © 1999 by *Tradeshow Week*®, Los Angeles, CA (323) 965-5335. Reprinted with permission.)

Consumer Shows

Broadly, consumer shows are open to the general public, who pay an admission charge. Exhibitors sell directly to the public; thus, this is retail trade between the exhibitor and the attendee. This type of show represents an expanding market for the consumer-based companies. Attendees actually take the product they buy home with them from the show floor. The trend is for companies to introduce new products and improve public relations efforts at these shows. Two of the best-known examples of consumer shows are the home and garden and auto shows.

For the convenience of the general working public, most consumer shows are held on weekends, or will last three to four days, starting on a Thursday and ending on a Sunday. They compete with all other entertainment attractions for the general public's entertainment budget.

Industry Shows

Industry, or trade (meaning "for the trade"), shows are open only to those individuals and companies that deal in the trade of a specific industry; they are closed to the public. Wholesale trade is the primary focus.

Exhibitors at these shows are distributors or wholesalers. Attendees must be "prequalified" through verification at the time of registration. They are generally members of an industry or trade association and must show proof of their status as professionals in the given industry.

Industry shows are usually held annually or semi-annually and last three to four days, though some extend to seven or ten days. Often, they are held in conjunction with a convention. The Super Show and COMDEX are familiar examples of these shows.

Horizontal Shows

As its directional name implies, a horizontal show highlights all products from a specific industry. For example, a hardware store show would feature exhibitors displaying nails, paint, plumbing equipment, gardening tools, electrical equipment, fencing, lawnmowers, and more. A grocery store show would be even more inclusive, offering not just foodstuffs, but video rental, motor oil, food preparation equipment, hosiery, cosmetics, and more. Today's grocery stores provide seemingly limitless buying and selling options.

Vertical Shows

In contrast to a horizontal show, a vertical show highlights a specific product for a specific industry. So a hardware store show might proffer hammers and nails only. There would be every type of hammer and nail, and products that support them, but it would be just hammers and nails. A vertical grocery store show might display only fruits.

Consolidation Shows

As the name implies, consolidation shows are open to both the general public and industry buyers or wholesalers. As in the other shows, the exhibitors are distributors or manufacturers. However, though open to both the public and the trade, hours may be restricted, so that the "pros" are not on the floor at the same time as the general public. And usually the industry attendees see the show first. And when the public is allowed access, exhibitors make an area in their booths available for retail sales.

International Shows

Usually called "trade fairs," international shows typically last much longer than their national counterparts. They provide a great arena in which many countries can market a variety of products for export. U.S. companies are now beginning to look at marketing exports through trade fairs as a cost-effective way to move American products.

What's in a Name?

Keeping all the preceding divisions of show types in mind, it's important to point out that more frequently today there is some movement from one type to another, often depending on the health of the industry the show is featuring. This means, for example, if the given industry is flourishing and public sales are not required, industry shows will remain closed to the public. But if that same industry is in a downward cycle, the show manager may decide to open the show to the general public for part of the "run."

Another alternative is to "spin" a consumer show off the industry show. At one time, consumers shows were regarded by those engaged in industry shows as something done only by the desperate to make ends meet. Now consumer shows are held in higher regard and are growing at an incredible pace because they are proving profitable for exhibitors and show managers alike.

The Players in the Shows

As noted at the beginning of this chapter, one of the primary reasons trade shows are so successful is the human element, the opportunity they offer to bring people in face-to-face contact. However, thus far, the discussion has mentioned only in passing, within the context of the general definition of the scope of this industry, the people, the "players," who make these shows happen. Though Chapter Two defines in more detail who these players are, and Chapters Three through Eight examines each in turn, it's important to complete this chapter by at least introducing them.

There are six major players in the exhibition industry, all directly or indirectly dependent on each other. Though they all have specific areas of focus, for any one to be successful, they all must work as a team. The players in the exhibition game are: exposition managers, venue managers, general service contractors, exhibitors, attendees, and convention and visitors bureau staff.

There are also numerous subcontractors in these main categories. For example, contracting and decorating firms, exhibit design firms, advertising and public relations agencies, labor unions, shipping firms, travel agencies, airlines, professional organizations, destination management firms, and many others. As noted, the remainder of this book describes these groups in detail.

Conclusion

The future looks bright for the exposition industry. According to the Center for Exhibition Industry Research, the number of expositions doubled from 1979 to 1993 (see Figure 1.6 for a monthly breakdown from 1997); furthermore, the size of the shows, the number of exhibiting companies, and the number of cities building venues to host expositions

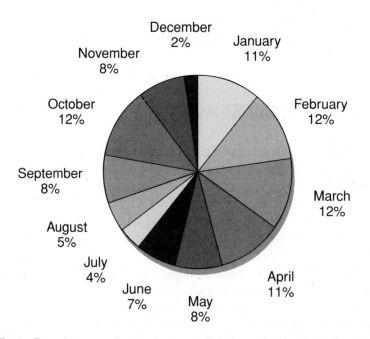

FIGURE 1.6 Expositions are held year-round, timed to coincide with industry buying season. Most exhibitions (45 percent) are held in the first quarter of the year. This pie chart shows 1997 U.S. exhibitions by month. (Source: © 1999 by *Tradeshow Week*®, Los Angeles, CA (323) 965-5335. Reprinted with permission.)

also doubled. More than 73 million people attend shows annually in the United States.

And remarkably, though this industry is cyclical, it can grow even during a down trend in the business community, because with business travel costs rising, corporate belts tightening, and reduced travel and entertainment budgets, face-to-face sales contacts still cost less than 50 percent than the average nonshow sales call.

ABC Trade Shows
EXHIBITOR

CHAPTER **2**

Defining the Players

The good news is, the trade show or exhibition industry has reached a new level of maturity and respect. But if it is to continue to grow and prosper, every industry employee will have to make the effort to understand not only every segment of this business, but also how it affects the industries most closely connected to it—travel, food service, hotels/lodging. No longer can a sophisticated exhibition be run just for the benefit of the attendees, exhibitors, venue, and exhibition management; an exposition's impact on a larger scale, that of the community in which it's held, must be considered as well.

Recall from Chapter One that we said the exposition industry traditionally has suffered from an "identity crisis," often misunderstood even by those who work in it or are closely linked to it. Certainly, to the general public, expositions just seem "to happen." Who organizes them? Steve Morello, president of the New York Convention & Visitors Bureau, has said "The perception of most people who visit a venue is that the venue owns, runs, and produces the show that is happening in their building or site. The public does not know that there are trade show managers that produce shows and may not even live in that city. The exhibitors train their own staff at varying degrees of customer service and also all the employees of the general service contractor." This chapter attempts to clarify exactly who is responsible for what in the production of a trade/consumer show.

Roll Call

The six major players in the exhibition industry were itemized in Chapter One; it is important to restate that they are all directly or indirectly dependent on one another, and thus comprise a *team*, which is responsible for the production of an exposition, or trade/consumer show. For convenience, here again is the list of players:

- Exhibition managers
- Exhibitors

Note

The strength of the exposition industry lies in the relationships and cooperation among these players.

- Venue managers and staff
- Convention and visitors bureau staff
- General service contractors
- Attendees

The role of each of these players will be defined in this chapter first as separate entities, then we will discuss their relationships and future of the industry. Subsequent chapters delve more fully into each, in turn.

Exposition Managers

The exposition manager can be considered the captain of the team. More than any of the other players, he or she must have the creative capabilities necessary to make the show unique and beneficial to both attendees and exhibitors. His or her responsibilities include the following:

- Conceptualize the show.
- Bring the other players together.
- Contract with the other players.
- Exhibitors

The exhibitors are the heart of any show. They are the individuals, groups, or companies that have the products, service, or ideas to sell or promote. Their responsibilities include:

- Lease exhibit floor space from the trade show manager.
- Set up and decorate their booth (if the show is in a non-unionized hall—this topic will be discussed later).
- Staff their booth and monitor visitor traffic.

- Work directly with the attendees to sell and/or promote goods, products, or services.
- Work with the convention and visitor's bureau if necessary to obtain hotel and restaurant reservations or entertainment suggestions.
- Contract with the venue manager and staff, if necessary, for utilities (necessary only if the venue manager contracts separately from the general service contractor).

Venue Managers and Staff

The venue is the building or other construct in which the exposition is held; the venue manager and staff are in charge of running the activities that take place within it. Generally, when people think of a trade/consumer show, they imagine a large convention hall, but a venue for an exposition can be almost any space and any size, indoor or outdoor, including a field, a parking lot, fairgrounds, a sports center, or a hotel or motel. A venue manager is responsible for the following:

- Generate new business.
- Work closely with the convention and visitor's bureau for leads from potential shows coming to the city.
- Increase revenue streams for the venue and community.
- Understand the needs and concerns of the customers and staff.
- Retain and manage quality staff.

Convention and Visitors Bureau Staff

Convention and visitors bureaus are the agencies that represent the hotels, services, and attractions in a venue site—usually a major city. Their involvement in the exposition industry is relatively new, but very important. The staff at these bureaus assist both exhibitors and the attendees. Their responsibilities include:

- Assist individuals and groups to book rooms.
- Make suggestions for dining and entertainment options.
- In general, make the visitors' experience a pleasant one, so that they can focus on their purpose—having a successful show.

- Coordinate continually with the exposition manager and venue manager to promote their city.
- In some cases, provide staff to the exposition manager to help with registration activities.

Metaphorically, these bureaus give show participants the key to their city, to make the entire experience as positive as possible. This benefits both the exposition representatives, by ensuring that the show is a complete success, and the city, by improving the chances that show groups will continue to use its facilities.

General Service Contractors

Once called decorators, the role of the general service contractor (GSC) has expanded along with the title. In brief, they supply the equipment and services necessary to ensure that the show runs smoothly. They:

- Supply the labor and equipment to decorate the venue.
- Design, install, and dismantle booths (if they are contracted to do so by the exhibitor, or if the show is in a unionized hall).

They do many "extras" to ease the work of the exhibitors and exposition mangers, such as finding vendors who will:

- Supply graphics for booths.
- Supply flowers for the hall.
- Supply cleaning services.
- Handle lighting, sound, staging, and audio-visual details.

Attendees

This player category is self-explanatory: Attendees are the trade/consumer show audience, the people who purchase or order products, goods, and services from the exhibitors, or at the very least gather information. Their "responsibilities" are:

- Pay registration or admission fees to gain access to the exposition.
- Book rooms.

- Eat in restaurants.
- Shop or visit attractions in venue location.
- In general, contribute to the local economy by spending money.

Attendees are not a single organized group, though a number of groups may (and often do) make up a significant percentage of the attendee population. Like all audiences, show attendees tend to be fickle, and so they must be "courted" by exposition managers and visitor and convention bureaus, or they will go somewhere else next year.

As you can see, each of these six players has a particular focus, and all are essential to the successful outcome of an exposition. Now that you've met them, let's examine how a show comes together.

Show Development and Contractual Arrangements

After the exposition manager creates the idea for a show, he or she must complete a number of steps necessary to make the show happen. Note that these steps may vary, depending on the specifics of the event; some may occur in a different order, while others may combine, but in general, this is how an exposition comes together.

The Exposition Manager's Steps to the Show Floor

1. The exposition manager selects the geographic location—the city—for the show.
2. The exposition manager may contact the location's convention and visitor's bureau for possible venues in that particular location or may directly contact various venues in the city that have been targeted for the show (usually the case when it's a repeat visit).
3. The exposition manager contracts with the venue manager to produce the show on the appropriate dates.
4. Advertising is launched, directed to potential exhibitors.
5. The exposition manager negotiates contracts with responding exhibitors for floor display space.

TABLE 2.1   Trade Show Players and Their Relationships

Trade Show Manager (TSM)	Venue Manager (VM)	Exhibitor	General Service Contractor (GSC)	Attendee	Convention Visitors Bureau (CVB)
VM	TSM	TSM	TSM	TSM	TSM
CSC	CVB	GSC	Exhibitor	Exhibitor	VM
CVB	Exhibitor*	CVB*	CVB*	CVB*	GSC
Exhibitor		Venue			Exhibitor*
Attendee					Attendee*

*Indicates that may not happen in all cases.

6. Advertising is launched to attract attendees. The type of advertisements and their timing is dependent upon whether the show is trade or consumer.

7. General service contractors submit proposals for supplying labor, equipment, and services to the exposition manager. The company with the winning bid is supplied with the names of the exhibitors.

8. A registration fee (for industry shows) or admission charge (for consumer shows) is determined by the exposition manager and collected from each attendee.

9. The venue manager contracts with the exposition manager at the show site for floor space based upon square footage. Note: Though the general service contractors do not contract with the venue, they must follow the rules and regulations of the venue so that during booth construction and decoration, they do not destroy or damage the venue in any way. The venue management works directly with the exhibitors only if the venue is charging the exhibitor for utilities—electricity, water, or gas.

10. The exhibitors contract with the exposition manager for exhibit space.

11. The general service contractors contract with exhibitors regarding their booth decoration requirements.

12. The attendees come to the show and, hopefully, spend money. Their spending activity is what pays all of the other players' salaries.

Table 2.1 summarizes how these players work together to produce a show.

Conclusion

As is common in most professions, the players in the exposition industry have formed associations to assist professionals in their field with education, information, and coordination with member colleagues. This chapter concludes with a representative list of those organizations.

Exposition, Trade Show, Managers Convention Liaison
Council (CLC)
1575 Eye St. NW
Washington, DC 20005
202-676-2764
Fax: 202-408-9652

International Association of Exposition Management (IAEM)
P.O. Box 802425
Dallas, TX 75389
972-458-8002
Fax: 972-458-8119

American Society of Association Executives (ASAE)
1575 Eye St.
Washington, DC 20005
202-626-2723
Fax: 202-371-8825

National Association of Consumer Shows (NACS)
147 S.E. 102nd Ave.
Portland, OR 97216
800-728-6227
503-253-0832
Fax: 503-253-9172

Meeting Planners International (MPI)
4455 LBJ Freeway, Suite 1200
Dallas, TX 75244-5903
214-746-5222
Fax: 214-702-6000

Professional Convention Management Association (PCMA)
100 Vestavia Office Park, Suite 220
Birmingham, AL 35216
205-823-7262
Fax: 205-822-3891
www.pcma.org

Canadian Association of Exposition Managers (CAEM)
International Centre, 6900 Airport Rd., Suite 239A
Box 82
Mississauga, ON L4V 1E8
Canada
905-678-9377
Fax: 905-678-9578

Religious Conference Management Association (RCMA)
One RCA Dome, Suite 120
Indianapolis, IN 46225
317-632-1888
Fax: 317-632-7909

Society of Independent Show Organizers (SISO)
P.O. Box 949
Framingham, MA 01701-0949
508-270-2640
Fax: 508-270-2642

Venue Managers

International Association of Assembly Managers (IAAM)
4425 W. Airport Freeway #590
Irving, TX 75022
972-255-8020
Fax: 972-255-9582

International Association of Conference Centers (IACC)
243 Lindbergh Blvd.
St. Louis, MO 63141-7851
314-993-8575
Fax: 314-993-8919

World Trade Centers Association (WTCA)
One World Trade Center, Suite 7701
New York, NY 10046

General Service Contractors

Exposition Service Contractors Association (ESCA)
Union Station, 400 S. Houston St., Suite 210
Dallas, TX 75202
214-742-9217
214-741-2519
www.ESCA.org

Convention and Visitors Bureaus

International Association of Convention & Visitors Bureaus
    (IACVB)
2000 L. St. NW, Suite 702
Washington, DC 20036-4990
202-296-7888
Fax: 202-296-7889
www.iacvb.org

Exhibitors Trade Show Exhibitors Association (TSEA)
5501 Backlick Rd., Suite 105
Springfield, VA 22151
703-941-3725
703-941-8275

ABC Trade Shows
EXHIBITOR

CHAPTER **3**

Exposition Manager

A trade or consumer show starts with an idea, and the exposition manager is the person who generates that idea. This chapter covers the questions that must be answered before taking steps to get the show on the show floor.

Once the focus for the show has been established, the exposition manager must identify who will make up the audience for the show. Without a clear understanding of a show's attendees, any trade or consumer show is doomed to fail, because, simply, without the appropriate audience to buy the products, goods, and services, the show will generate little or no profit for the rest of the players.

To identify precisely who a show's attendees are, the exposition manager must ask a series of questions:

1. Who and how big is my audience?
2. How much will they be willing to spend to attend this show?
3. What types of exhibitors do they want and need to see?
4. How many days, on average, will they spend at the show?
5. How can I make this show new and exciting for the audience?
6. Will this show attract local, regional, national, or international exhibitors?
7. Will the attendees be local, regional, national, or international?
8. What time of the year is best to hold this show?
9. What part of the country or world is most convenient and/or appealing to the attendees?

The exposition manager will make different contractual arrangements based on the type of show being organized:

- *Management companies.* These companies typically contract with a trade or industry association to run their annual or biannual show. The management company is paid a flat rate, in addition to payment based on space sales and attendance.
- *Association staff.* If a trade association itself is organizing a show, it will usually have its own year-round staff assigned to producing

the show, meetings, or conventions. In this way, the association staff takes over as the exposition manager.

- *Entrepreneurs.* These private businesspeople are responsible for running a show, and are limited only by their imagination and fiscal resources. As with association staff, entrepreneurs would act as exposition managers.

Trade or Consumer

To review, there are two main categories of shows: trade and consumer. Combinations are formed from these two, and they will be discussed later.

Trade Shows

Remember, the trade, or industry, show is private, that is, not open to the general public. It is designed for the professionals who work in a specific industry, the exhibitors that service that industry, and the attendees, the buyers, from that specific industry. Logically then, trade shows offer products for wholesale value, rather than retail.

Because attendance is limited to trade members only, preregistration is required to verify that attendees are qualified. To qualify, they show proof of membership in a trade association or a license to work in the given industry. Trade show attendees generally can be expected to come from all over the country and stay for the duration of the show, typically four days and three nights in a hotel as close to the show site as possible.

A familiar example of a trade show is the Super Show, the largest sporting goods apparel exposition in the country. Most major sporting goods companies set up exhibit booths to offer their wares to retailers that sell sporting goods to the general public. Exhibitors include such brand names as Nike, Reebok, and Wilson, supplying retailers ranging from such discount giants as Kmart and Wal-Mart to local tennis and golf pro shops. In essence, then, the attendees of a trade show are retailers. Most sales comprise large product orders, which are later shipped from the exhibitor's manufacturer to the retailer-attendee. Products are not generally taken off the show floor.

Did You Know?

Though most trade shows attract attendees from all over the United States, more frequently today, many also bring in an international audience.

Advertising for trade shows is done primarily through association membership mailing lists and industry-specific (that is, trade) publications. This is highly targeted advertising, directed at qualified buyers.

Consumer Shows

A consumer show is open to the general public, meaning that anyone who can afford the entrance fee can gain entrance to the show. Consumer shows usually offer a wide range of products for sale on the show floor; and in the case of smaller products, attendees usually take their purchases home with them. The exhibitors, then, are essentially retailers selling to the general public, in much the same way as doing business from stores.

Common types of consumer shows include home and garden, boat, flower, and auto shows. (Note that because consumer shows often display large products such as boats and cars, it takes more time to set up and dismantle them. On average, it takes 5.4 days to set up a large-product consumer show and 2.7 days to dismantle it, in comparison to smaller-product shows, which take, on average, 1 day to set up and 1 day to dismantle.

More often than not, consumer shows attract regional audiences, so attendees frequently drive or use public transportation to travel to the show; and rarely do they make use of hotel accommodations, and then usually for one night only.

Promotion and advertising for consumer shows are done through mainstream, traditional media—radio, television, and newspapers—though direct mail is sometimes also used (for example, for a boat show, owners of speed boats or yacht club members might be mailed a show announcement).

Historically, consumer shows have been regarded by many in the trade show sector as less desirable, because, typically, they do not

Megashows

Megashows refer to exhibitions that contract for space of more than 500,000 square feet and attract more than 70,000 attendees. Familiar megashows include COMDEX, the Super Show, Consumer Electronics Show (CES), MAGIC (Men's Apparel Guild In California), Food Marketing Institute (FMI), and the National Hardware Show (NHS).]

For shows of this magnitude to continue to be successful, they must constantly reinvent themselves. They must regularly analyze and evaluate the show from the attendee and exhibitor standpoints to improve. In other words, a megashow's organizers must keep one eye on the future and the other on its current base of exhibitors and attendees.

The primary concern of all megashow managers is that even in the midst of the enormity of the exposition, attendees and exhibitors be made to feel a part of the show, that in some way they "own" it; otherwise, they will get lost in traffic. It is important to point out that megashows do not compete with other megashows, which are geared to entirely separate industries; rather, their competition is the smaller vertical, or specialized, show. Therefore, megashow organizers must find ways to help attendees locate exhibitors they are looking for quickly and efficiently. Some megashow planners will even research the buying patterns of their attendees and place exhibitors on the floor that are closely related to each other so that attendees only have to navigate a small portion of the show floor. In venues comprising more than one exhibit space, buyers of related products from major corporations will be placed in the same exhibit hall.

Likewise, megashow managers must maintain positive relationships with their exhibitors to ensure that they will continue to lease space year after year. Most show management will assign staff to check in with their exhibitors two to three times per year. They dedicate staff to facilitating the exhibitors' experience at the show. The staff will send attendee lists to the exhibitors prior to the show so that the exhibitors may send notifications in advance of the products they intend to exhibit, to encourage more traffic. This, coupled with the general trade show promotion, helps to attract the widest possible audience.

Megashow managers must also stay in close contact with the industry at all times to detect trends, so as to keep their exhibitors and attendees current, or one step ahead, of their competition. The megashow manager must have a five- to ten-year plan of growth for the show, including expanding the attendee base. Where will these new attendees come from? Today, most megashow managers work with the Department of Commerce's (DOC) International Buyers Program to attract international buyers. The DOC is concerned with the balance of trade, and to attract international buyers to a U.S. trade show enhances the number of our exports to other countries.

The media is a great source of promotion for megashows. Frequently, for example, major television network morning news programs will broadcast live from a car or electronics show.

generate as much revenue for the venue city—travel, lodging, food service, and so on—because the attendees, as noted, are frequently local. Consequently, convention centers and visitors bureaus have not pursued consumer shows for their venues as actively as they have the trade shows.

More recently, however, many in the exposition industry have come to realize that consumer shows have a greater economic impact than previously thought, arguing that it is difficult to accurately determine how much of a city's hospitality resources are being tapped by attendees of these shows because they do not preregister. Therefore, tracking where they come from, where they stay and/or eat, and what entertainment they might take advantage of is nearly impossible. But it is known that attendance at some consumer shows can climb to more than 1.4 million attendees. And the demographics tend to be much younger; the average age of a trade show attendee is 47, while the average age of the consumer show attendee is 19, an age group thought to spend more on food and entertainment.

Furthermore, the ratio of attendees to exhibitors at consumer expositions is much higher than at trade shows. The 1993 *Trade Show Week Date Book* reveals that the ratio of attendees to exhibitors at consumer shows averages 63 to 1, whereas the ratio of attendees to exhibitors at trade shows averages 25 to 1. Note, however, that the ratio goes up at trade shows that are also open to consumers (91 to 1). The ratio of attendees to exhibitors at the 10 largest consumer expositions was an outstanding 444 to 1.

Horizontal or Vertical

To recap from Chapter One, both consumer and trade shows may be organized as *horizontal* or *vertical* in scope, determined by the exhibitors that are included or excluded. Specifically, at a horizontal show, all the products considered part of an industry would be eligible for inclusion. Recall from Chapter One the example of a horizontal show for the grocery industry. Exhibits at such a show could include: fruits, vegetables, meats, household cleaning products, cosmetics, cards and gift wrap, automotive do-it-yourself products, videos, and any of the other myriad products found in today's superstores.

In contrast, the vertical grocery show would be limited to, say, just produce. All types of produce would be eligible for inclusion, but *only* produce and perhaps a limited number of closely related products.

There are advantages and disadvantages to both vertical and horizontal trade shows, listed here.

Horizontal Show Advantages

- Attendees see a wide and full range of products.
- Generally, show profits are better, because maximum booth space is sold.
- The audience is more diverse and therefore usually larger.
- The horizontal show is often the most important and largest of the year in the particular industry.

Horizontal Show Disadvantages

- Attendees may feel overwhelmed by the huge number of products, particularly if the show is unfocused or poorly laid out and organized.
- The show may be too big, in which case, many attendees will get tired and give up before they see all the products.
- Though there are large numbers of exhibitors, there may not be enough of a certain type of exhibitor to enable attendees to comparison-shop a particular product.

Vertical Show Advantages

- Attendees can compare a specific product offered by many different companies.
- Because they are smaller, vertical shows are easier to navigate; attendees usually manage to see all the products and feel less confused about what they've seen later.

Vertical Show Disadvantages

- Attendee traffic may be light, attracting only a select few to see the limited product types.
- Lighter traffic means less floor space sold, and fewer product sales generated, all resulting in lower total show profits.

Location, Location, Location

Those who work in real estate often say the three most important factors in the business are location, location, and location. In the exposition industry, location—the city and venue—is almost as important. So once the exposition manager has defined the show, the next questions he or she must answer are: Where should we hold the show? In which city and at which venue?

Choosing the City

First, the region of the country must be determined, keeping in mind of course the show dates, because weather can make or break a show; inclement weather can delay or prevent exhibitors (and their equipment and products) and attendees from reaching the site. For example, planning a show in Chicago during the winter is probably not a good idea. That said, when a show budget is tight, sometimes holding a show in a city during its "off-season" can mean price breaks for venue leases, hotel rates, and so on. The exposition manager will have to balance all factors to make the decision.

Choosing the Venue

Most "show cities" have more than one venue option, so once the exposition manager has selected the city, the next step is to review the available convention centers, show halls, hotel ballrooms, coliseums, auditoriums, and any other sites that might be suitable. Managers should not overlook less traditional spaces; an unusual site can be a plus, making the show more interesting and appealing to attendees, who often attend numerous such shows.

Many factors comprise venue evaluation. The exposition manager should get answers to these questions:

- Where in the city is the venue located? Is it easily accessible from the airport and via other transportation? Is it in a safe part of town?
- How big is the venue, in square feet?
- Is the size adequate for the show currently being planned, and is there room for growth for future shows?

- What is the charge per square foot?
- What other costs will the venue charge exhibitors and the show manager?
- Are the loading docks and the load capacity of the floors adequate for exhibitors' booths?
- Is the venue union or nonunion? Will either of these situations be a deterrent for your exhibitors?
- Does the venue have a good reputation? What other shows have been held there? (Ask for and follow up on recommendations from other show managers who have worked with the venue.)
- Is there sufficient venue staff available? Are they efficient, knowledgeable, and easy to work with?
- Are there any political situations currently disrupting the city or surrounding areas that might impact the association, organization, or attendees of that show?
- How many other shows will be going on at other venues at the same time, causing overbooking at hotels, restaurants, and entertainment sites; difficulty accessing transportation; and so on.

Show Staff

Once the city and the venue are fixed, the exposition manager must make staff assignments and estimate how much extra help will be needed to produce the show. Without the right people in the right jobs, nothing will get done on time or properly. The manager deals with two employee groups: *exposition management employees* and *outsource providers*. (Figure 3.1 shows a typical organizational flowchart of the coordination among show staff members.)

Exposition Management Employees

The exposition manager's in-house staff must share his or her overall vision and understanding of the show, even though they will be divided into various departments that handle specific tasks and may not work all that closely with each other on a daily basis. Each task is integral to the success of the entire show, so though working separately, they must be united in focus.

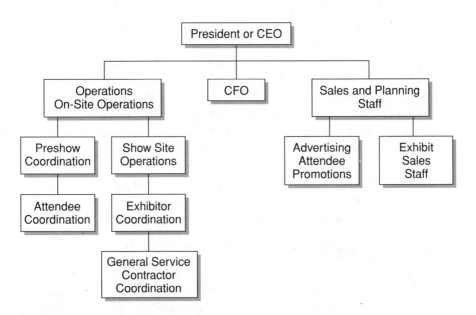

FIGURE 3.1 Organization for Best Show Ever, Inc.

Outsource Providers/Consultants

In general, the exposition manager must depend on outsource providers, independent professionals who do not work for the trade association or professional organization producing the show. They include firms providing housing, exhibit booth sales, registration, site selection, contract negotiation, meeting planning, show management, transportation, drayage, and more. Exposition Managers do not have to be expert in all areas of the show. As the industry expands and becomes more complex, the need for experts in these new niches becomes more important—a consultant or outsource provider becomes essential. This may appear confusing, but a show manager may contract with each of these services individually instead of contracting these services through a general services contractor.

The huge growth in the '80s and '90s of the number of independent contractors, caused by widespread corporate downsizing and reengineering, means that show managers have many more professionals to choose from to meet the needs of show production. But it also means that they must take more time and pay very close attention to evaluating and reviewing expertise.

The growing number of independent contractors also has raised problems regarding the pricing of services. Is a flat fee the way to go? Or will it be more cost-effective to pay hourly or daily rates? And what about commissions, retainers, and percentages of event costs? The bottom line is, the exposition manager must determine in advance of any work how services will be billed and paid for. When an independent contractor is engaged for a show, they may be involved in operations or sales and marketing. If the work is based on sales performance then the contract should be based on sales. If it is not, then the contract should specify an hourly or per project rate.

Promoting the Show

To have a successful show requires highly motivated and qualified attendees to buy from a full range of qualified and well-suited exhibitors. Perhaps two of the most difficult responsibilities of the exposition manager are, one, estimating the number and, two, analyzing the type of exhibitors and attendees that will make the event financially successful—not just for the current year, but for subsequent shows as well.

One source for determining these statistics is registration data from previous shows, containing attendee demographics and psychographics useful for establishing trends in space sales, types of exhibitors, and more. Like successful companies in any industry that continually analyze their customer base to ensure they are providing the best possible products and services, exposition managers must know exactly who their "customers" are.

Once the exposition manager has determined who the audience is, he or she should have the show staff prepare and send to all potential exhibitors a list of registered attendees, four to five months

Did You Know?

The industry term for attendee research and advertising is *attendance promotion*.

in advance of the show. This gives exhibitors ample time to merge the attendee list with their current client lists and to send a mailing announcing their presence at the show and inviting attendees to schedule time to stop by.

Another useful method that show managers use to maintain updated statistics is to survey attendees and exhibitors during the current show, to determine their interests and purpose, and to learn their suggestions and/or complaints. Surveys are taken from the attendees and exhibitors both prior to and after the show. A show manager will survey exhibitors either about the logistics of their booth and of the show floor, or about the attendees' buying activities. The attendee can be surveyed at registration and on the show floor, or through a direct mail campaign. They are generally asked their opinions of site selection, willingness to return to the show, buying/purchasing habits, and reason for attending the show. Subsequently making survey results available to exhibitors will assist them in improving sales, thus making the show as a whole more profitable; and, ideally, leading to exhibitors committing to next year's show, with requests for expanded floor space.

On-site Promotion

The on-site advertising and promotion that the exposition manager and staff do during a show is very important for the exhibitors. It might include a program of events, talks, and entertainment; guides; a floor plan and list of the exhibitors. Other typical offerings are "show dailies," magazines produced on-site by the trade magazine publishers that attend the show. These publications highlight the daily happenings at the show; announce new product innovations, late-breaking news from industry leaders; excerpt interviews with speakers and celebrities at the show; and provide another resource for advertising the show.

More recent advertising innovations are audio billboards and "convention television." Exhibitors may buy space on the billboards to attract attendees; they play continuously, announcing the locations and sales incentives of featured exhibitors. Convention television runs both taped programs, giving in-depth coverage of a company or industry personage, and on-the-spot programming from the show floor, where reporters interview exhibitors and attendees.

Press coverage is essential to the success of a show for both the exposition manager and the exhibitors. The expo manager should ensure that:

- Show and exhibitor press kits are distributed.
- The press room is set up. This should be an area where the press can work comfortably. The room must, of course, be equipped to accommodate phones, fax machines, computers, and so on.
- Press conferences are scheduled.
- Press parties are organized to acquaint the press with attendees and exhibitors.
- Press contact lists are distributed to exhibitors so that they can pursue media coverage of their products/services and companies.
- Media are given exhibitors for interviews.

This is only a partial list of the kinds of services the exposition manager has to arrange for in order to generate positive relationships between the press and the show participants.

Post-Show Promotion

After the show has closed, the exposition manager's responsibility to the exhibitors is not over. He or she should continue to serve them by making available to all exhibitors a complete list of attendees broken down by name, title, name of company, product/service, geographical region, and so on, which the exhibitors can use later for mailing campaigns or special sales strategies. It is important that the expo manager give the exhibitors as much information as possible to assist them in reaching their audience, thus making it more likely that the exhibitors will be repeat participants in future shows. In this way, both "players" win.

The Show Floor

Exposition management is a service position, thus it is the exposition manager's job to serve all segments of the industry that is the focus of the trade show under development. To that end, the exposition manager must oversee the design of the venue to transform it into a veritable marketplace for retail or wholesale sales.

Floor Plan

The trade show floor *is* the marketplace, and the manager must make sure it is laid out for efficiency as well as ambiance. If attendees are confused by the floor plan, or thwarted by "traffic jams" at crucial aisle crossings, or dumbfounded by booth positioning, chances are they won't hang around long enough to buy anything. The floor plan must be an enhancement to the show experience, not a stumbling block. Furthermore, the show floor is the profit center of the show, so the show manager must draw up the floor plan to make the best financial use of the space. Figure 3.2 is a sample floor plan for an exhibit hall containing 10 foot by 10 foot booths.

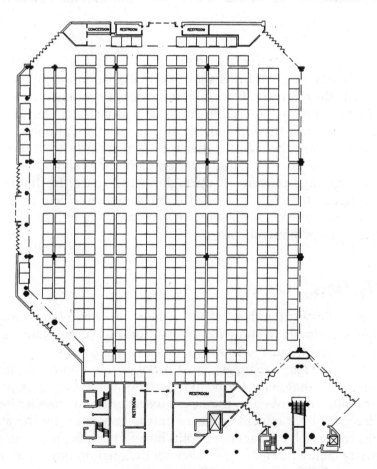

FIGURE 3.2   Sample floor plan. (Source: Georgia World Congress Center)

Did You Know?

There's a simple formula you can use to figure out the number of gross square feet you need at a venue. Multiply the equivalent number of 10 foot by 10 foot booths by 100 square feet, then add the amount of square footage needed for special areas; this will give you the net square footage. Double the net to get the gross. If, for example, you require 50,000 square feet net for exhibit booths and special booths, you will need approximately 100,000 gross square feet. But keep in mind that this calculation will be affected by other factors, including fire regulations, utilities, and other venue rules (see the "Safety First" sidebar later in this chapter).

In the case of a consumer show, particular attention must be paid to facilitate the opportunity for the audience to experience the show in its entirety, meaning entertainment as well as product viewing. Simply put, the longer the consumer is motivated to remain on the show floor, the greater the chances that they will contribute to the profit of the event by buying. Thus, entertainment areas should be spread out to encourage movement throughout the space. In this regard, managers can take the lead from retail stores that have positioned merchandise so that the customer is automatically exposed at every turn to displays of merchandise.

Traffic Flow

Obviously, heavy attendee "traffic"—the number of people viewing a booth—is desirable to show exhibitors. But if the floor plan has been poorly designed, causing traffic tie-ups, everyone loses.

The trade show manager must make design booth assignments in such a way that helps traffic to flow. This is done by interspersing *anchor booths* (described in the next subsection) with smaller booths. Smaller exhibitors benefit from the traffic generated by the anchor booths; conversely, the anchor booths benefit from the lesser amounts of activity taking place in the smaller booths surrounding them, which of course helps to even out traffic.

Display Design

Display design incorporates exhibitor booths, registration or admissions areas, food service areas, exhibitor lounges, attendee rest areas, press rooms, and trade or association information areas.

Booth Types

We define booth types in greater detail in Chapter Four, but for the purposes of this discussion, here are three primary categories:

> *Anchor booths.* Large, well-lit exhibits set up by major and/or most familiar companies in the industry. They usually feature entertainment, music, and/or food, and are staffed by a large number of company representatives.
>
> *In-line booths.* The majority of booths are in-line, that is, within the rows, not on a corner or end. Typically used by smaller exhibitors, in-line booths measure approximately 10 feet by 10 feet or 10 feet by 20 feet.
>
> *Corner booths.* Two-sided booths on row "corners." The show manager can charge double for a corner booth because it has two sides exposed to traffic. It is estimated that an exhibitor has seven seconds to attract the attention of an attendee; however, corner booths are regarded as providing fourteen seconds of exposure, hence the higher price for the space.

Dollars and Sense

Though left until the end of this chapter, money questions are hardly the least important the exposition manager must answer. Indeed, it is essential that he or she establish a budget in order to set appropriate boundaries and limitations for the show, otherwise more may go out (expenses) than come in (income), spelling disaster for the show.

The first, broad, question the manager should ask is: What is the financial goal for the show? Can it show a profit, or at least break even, in its first year? To find this answer, it is necessary to compare income with expenses, as in any other budget.

Safety First

In assessing a venue's usable square footage, it is imperative to be cognizant of local fire regulations, which vary throughout the country, and therefore should be carefully studied. The local fire marshall is responsible for ensuring the safety of everyone at the show, and if there is any doubt about the safety of your floor plan, it is conceivable that your show may be closed or delayed until all regulations are met.

Fire regulations usually require a specified amount of unobstructed footage for the following:

- Width of aisles, both standard and major cross-aisles.
- From entrances and exits.
- From all fire hydrants.
- From all fire extinguishers.
- Surrounding all columns.

Regulations also stipulate:

- Equipment safety standards.
- Adequate access to restrooms and drinking fountains.
- Lobby signage and other registration requirements.
- Adequate sight lines to exits.
- Inflammable booth construction materials.
- Precautions for vehicles.

Once floor plans for a show have been drawn, they must be submitted to the local fire department for approval, generally in blueprint form. Your approved plan is your first line of defense in case of legal action resulting from any accidents or injuries.

Income

The following comprise income sources for the exposition manager:

- *Booth space sales.* This is the largest single area of profit for show managers. Booth space is sold by the square foot, the total of which then determines the size of the show and cash flow prior to its opening. The number of exhibitors becomes the incentive that entices attendees to come, which in turn generates registrations or admission revenue.

- *Registration and/or admission fees.* This is the second largest area for profit. This is a highly variable revenue depending upon these factors: (1) the current economic status of the industry that the show is representing. Obviously, if an industry is in a down period, fewer people will exhibit at or attend the show. However, this does not necessarily mean an unsuccessful show, because those who do attend usually are "qualified to purchase" at the show. So though there may be fewer attendees, exhibitors may write as many orders as if the show floor were packed . (2) Effectiveness of preshow promotions and advertising. (3) Mother Nature, the great variable, which even the most experienced show manager cannot predict. Terrible weather prevents attendees from driving or flying to a city; it may even cause exhibitor product shipments to be delayed.

- *Corporate sponsorships.* Often, trade shows seek to improve their bottom line by gaining sponsorship dollars during the show. Sponsorships can also lend credibility to a show, a less tangible, but no less important generator of profit in the form of cost savings and/or enhancements to productivity and efficiency. Sponsorships may come in the form of cash or "in-kind services," which include, for example, the use of equipment at no charge, advertisements, promotions, loan of staff, or the use of products.

- *Food and beverages.* This income area is dependent upon whether the show is being held in a venue that allows the manager to contract with private food and beverage contractors or an exclusive caterer. And, if alcohol is served, this can become a major source of income for a show manager.

- *Parking.* A particularly good source of income from consumer shows, many of whose attendees drive to the show. More commonly, with industry or trade shows attendees fly to the show city and use cabs or shuttle services to the venue, though some parking income is generated from a number of attendees who rent cars.

Expenses

An exposition manager's first expense is hiring his or her staff. As discussed in the "Staff" section, a number of different professions are required to produce a show. Staff who deal with contracting with exhibitors should be the first to be hired. They work year-round to, first, attract exhibitors and, second, to coordinate with them as the show date nears. In most cases, this remains a small staff until a few months prior to the show, when, usually, temporary help is added. Show staffs can increase from 2 full-time employees to as many as 16 staff assistants. The average is 7 to 9 in the office.

Staff, depending on size, will also be responsible for promoting the show; and for industry shows, they will also handle registration and direct mail.

The following lists break out the most common areas of expenses and income that an exposition manager must consider:

EXPENSES

General Exposition

- Lease/rent for exhibit hall or venue
- Exposition decorations
- Legal advice for and preparation of exhibitor contracts
- Exhibitor meeting, office, lounge areas
- Trash removal
- Utility charges
- Storage (for shipping crates)
- Registration equipment and personnel
- Press room setup
- Audiovisual equipment

Personnel

- Pre- and postshow help
- Security
- Travel, food lodging

Printing and Promotion

- Programs and maps
- Badges
- Registration forms
- Bus and other transportation schedules

- Print advertising
- Direct mail
- Public relations materials

Equipment

- Booth, to promote show and use during the show
- Signage
- Office furniture and equipment for show site
- Press room equipment
- General office supplies

Miscellaneous

- Insurance
- Taxes
- Shipping
- Postage
- Shuttle service for attendees

INCOME

- Advance ticket sales
- Registration and admissions
- Exhibit booth sales
- Parking
- Corporate sponsorships
- Special events or banquets

Timing Is Everything

It should be clear by now that trade shows do not happen overnight. The rule of thumb is to begin planning two years in advance, tracking trends in the industry and surveying former exhibitors and attendees. Then, one year in advance, specific tasks should be laid out month by month, as delineated in the "calendar" below.

Note

The time line for a consumer show is the same for an industry show, except that advertising directed to attendees is launched only in the 45 days prior to the show's opening, usually using local and regional television, radio, and newspaper formats.

The following monthly breakdown assigns deadlines the exposition manager must meet for a show occurring in November.

December

- Sign contracts with convention center and hotels.
- Select the general services manager.
- Send first mailing to prospective exhibitors.

January

- Send first press release to trade press and other media, as appropriate.

February

- Send first announcements or other incentives to exhibitors to enhance sales of booth space.

March

- Send second round of announcements to exhibitors.
- Hire security company.

April

- Send follow-up press releases.
- Finalize the arrangements for special guests or promotions for the show.
- Study other shows to generate potential exhibitors.

May

- Finalize transportation arrangements (buses, shuttles) for attendees.
- Select registration company.
- Initialize lists of attendees.

June

- Send another mailing to prospective exhibitors.
- Design preregistration materials.
- Confirm hotel arrangements.
- Prepare site locator maps.
- Establish show hours, social and food functions.
- Confirm parking facilities, exposition telephone number(s), show office telephone number and address.
- Finalize expo floor plan.

July–August

- Send third mailing to exhibitors, including sponsorship opportunities, educational programs (if any), and show directory information and advertising opportunities.
- Send fourth mailing to press, updating expo events.
- Send first program mailing to attendees.

September

- Send exhibitor kits.
- Send reminder cards to attendees.
- Send fifth media new releases.

October

- Order directional and booth signs from general services contractor.
- Make final arrangements with hotels, security, service contractors and caterers.

- Notify media of photo opportunities and show dates/times.
- Send follow-up direct mail promotions to attendees.

November

- Align registration company and/or expo staff on-site to register attendees and supervise show setup.
- Troubleshoot.
- Survey attendees and exhibitors for next year.

December

- Evaluate expo; make recommendations for future shows and show growth based on the number of attendees and number and type of exhibitors.
- Compile final show performance report.

Conclusion

No doubt about it, an exposition manager's job is complex and multi-faceted. Throughout the year, ongoing analysis of the event provides trend information enabling the manager to make long-term goals and set the direction for future shows. Ideally, the manager will outline a business plan that begins with goal-setting. It is recommended that two or three major goals be set for each show—goals that are attainable yet challenging enough to ensure that growth and improvement are continual; for example, to increase booth sales by 15 percent or a dollar amount, or to increase attendee levels by a certain percentage. Another important goal is to expand the types of exhibitors to keep the show fresh and innovative.

Naturally, these goals should be followed by the actions necessary to take to ensure their fruition. In summation, it's safe to say that an exposition manager's job is never done.

CHAPTER 4

Exhibitors

We've said it before, but it bears repeating: If enough exhibitors do not buy booth space and set up displays, there will be no show. Their commitment and creativity make or break a show. For exhibitors, participation in trade shows is economically sound; it is cheaper and more effective than sending salespeople out in the field. In addition, exhibitors buy space at such a show to:

- Target prequalified buyers.
- Meet buyers face to face.
- Demonstrate new products.
- Obtain product/service feedback.
- Improve customer relations.
- Conduct market research.
- Educate dealers.
- Take advantage of "action-oriented" media.
- Identify market direction.
- Develop sales leads.
- Generate positive, or overcome unfavorable, publicity.
- Promote product trends.
- Answer customer concerns or complaints.

Exhibitors will only be interested in buying booth space when they are assured of an appropriate and adequate audience base; they will want to know, "will there be enough attendees who are qualified to buy?" In part, they gain this assurance from the trade show manager, who, as you learned in Chapter Three, develops a thorough understanding of the audience the show intends to attract, before he or she begins to promote a show to potential exhibitors. For example, in a food service industry show, it might seem obvious that attendees would be interested in seeing exhibitors that represent companies that manufacture large and small kitchen appliances, tableware, uniforms, menus, lighting, dining furniture, and so on. But the show manager must think more broadly, and recognize that attendees might also need contact with exhibitors who, for example, sell daily planners, outdoor signage, or accounting software packages, or who are financial and vacation planners and retirement specialists.

However, the trade show manager's assessment of the audience should not be enough for exhibitors; they should do their own evaluation of the audience and its potential for their companies.

Evaluating the Audience and Audience Potential

Questions that an exhibitor must find the answers to before signing a contract to purchase booth space at a show are: What are my objectives for exhibiting at this show? What is the potential for meeting those objectives at this show? We talk more about defining other objectives later in the chapter, but for now it's important to understand that, almost without exception, the most important objective is to reach a targeted customer. Therefore, exhibitors must determine whether the show's attendees comprise the correct consumer base for their product(s) or service(s). Do those attendees have the buying authority and the budget to order a particular product within a time period that meets the company's sales goals?

To evaluate an audience, an exhibitor should follow these steps:

1. *Obtain attendee numbers from previous shows (if available), along with predicted numbers for the upcoming show.* These figures should be available from the exposition manager or a member of his or her staff. These numbers are the basis for the rest of the audience evaluation process.

2. *Obtain an attendee profile from the exposition manager or member of his or her staff.* Make sure you receive demographic (age, gender, education, profession, income, geographical location, etc.) as well as psychographic (buying patterns, attitudes toward the industry, motivations for decision making, etc.) information.

3. *Based on the information in step 1, calculate the potential of the audience.* If, say, 10,000 attendees are expected to come to the show and your attendee profile research concluded that 35 percent of that number would be interested in a particular product, the potential audience for that product and company would be $10,000 \times .35 = 3,500$.

4. *Ascertain whether the show is being set up as a vertical or horizontal show*. This is important information, because at a vertical show, the attendee is generally more focused, because the show is targeted to a narrower type of exhibitor.

If the results of this process are positive—that is, the exhibitor determines it would be worthwhile to participate in the show—the next step is to contract for booth space.

Signing On

As described in Chapter Three, the exposition manager is responsible for contracting with exhibitors for booth space. Figure 4.1 shows a sample exhibitor contract. Though there can be many specifics and variations in this type of contract, this sample includes the basics for this type of agreement.

Show Planning

Planning for the show is as important, if not more so, than what is accomplished during the show; in fact, planning is what determines what is (or is not) accomplished. For exhibitors, six months to a year is not too early to begin planning; the minimum is three months prior to the show date.

The show must be considered an essential marketing tool by all of the departments of the exhibiting company. Therefore, the same marketing principles for any promotional campaign apply. They are to:

1. Set objectives.
2. Determine a budget.
3. Design a system to measure performance and return on investment.
4. Plan show promotion.
5. Design the exhibit.
6. Train show team.

We'll delve into each of these in turn.

Exhibitor's Contract

This Agreement made and entered into this _____ day of _____ 19___, by and between The Best Show Ever, Inc. (Hereinafter referred to as "Show") and Sell It All Exhibitor (hereinafter referred to as the "Exhibitor").

WITNESSETH:

Whereas, Show has entered into a lease Agreement with the Everywhere in the World Convention Center (hereinafter referred to as "Convention Center"), for the use of the facility.

Whereas, the Exhibitor desires to lease exhibit space at the Convention Center, upon the conditions stated herein and subject to the Agreement between the Show and the Convention Center. It is expressly understood that space and space location is at the sole and complete discretion of the Show.

NOW, THEREFORE, the parties agree as follows:

1. *Exhibit area.* Show leases to the Exhibitor during the days of the show only the following space, to wit: booth-exhibit area: _____ Located as follows: _____.

2. *Purpose.* Exhibitor shall use said space for the following exhibit or display described as follows: _____ at the Convention Center, as the same may appear on the space plats of the Show.

3. *Rent.* The Exhibitor shall pay to the Show the agreed rental of $_____, payable on or before _____, and $_____ on or before _____.

4. *Refund.* In the event of cancellation for any reason, it is agreed that the exact damages to the Show would be difficult to ascertain and therefore all monies paid shall be retained as liquidated damages (i.e., no refunds).

5. *Show access.* The Show, its agents, or assigns shall have access to the aforesaid described space and premises at all times.

6. *Conduct.* The exhibitor shall conduct the operation of the exhibitor or display in a quiet and orderly manner at all times, and shall keep the exhibit area neat, clean, and free from rubbish.

7. *Sound Devices.* Exhibitor shall obtain permission from the Show for use in its exhibit or display all sound devices such as radios, speakers, stereo, organs, and any other attention-getting device, such that said use will not interfere with any other display or exhibit. The Show reserves the right to revoke permission for the use of such sound devices at any time for cause.

8. *Fire code.* Exhibitor shall obtain approval of the show and the fire marshall for any structure used in its exhibit or display.

9. *Structure size.* Displays erected within all exhibit buildings shall not exceed _____ feet in height at the back wall of the booth nor extend _____ feet

FIGURE 4.1   Sample exhibitor contract.

forward from the back wall at this height. Displays in the forward _____ feet of booth space shall not exceed _____ inches in height.

10. *Liability.* Exhibitor understands that it is an independent contractor and is not covered by the Show's workman's compensation insurance. The Exhibitor agrees to indemnify, and hold harmless, and defend the Show, its officers, agents, and employees from any and all claims, causes of action, any suits resulting from any damage, injury, or loss to any person or persons, including all persons to whom the Exhibitor may be liable under any workman's compensation law, social security law, and the contractor itself, from any loss, damage, cause of action, claims or suit for damages of any nature whatsoever, including but not limited to loss of property, goods, wares or merchandise, caused by or arising out of in any way, whatsoever connected with the exercise by Exhibitor of this Agreement, standard state workman's compensation and employers' liability, including occupational disease, covering all individuals engaged in performance of the work at the set-in amount required by state statutes: comprehensive general public liability and property damage insurance, including personal injury and products liability-bodily injury: $500,000 each occurrence; property damage, $500,000 each occurrence; $500,000 aggregate property damage.

11. *Display time.* Exhibitor agrees to have its exhibit or display in place _____ prior to the opening of the Show and remain intact until 10:00 p.m., _____ the final day of the Show.

12. *Laws.* The premises subleased herein shall be used according to the requirement set forth by the Show, Convention Center, and the state and federal laws, and without infringement upon the rights of others.

13. *Business Limits.* Exhibitor shall not engage in any other business whatsoever upon or within the Convention Center, except that which is herein expressly agreed to, and will confine all transactions to the space herein subleased.

14. *Changes.* There will be no change, alteration, variation, or deviation from the terms of the Agreement, unless made in writing and signed by all parties hereto, and that no verbal understanding or agreements, past, present, or future not incorporated herein shall be valid or binding on either party. It is further understood and agreed that all representations regarding this Agreement are contained herein and understood by the parties hereto.

15. *Assignment.* Neither party to this Agreement may assign its rights or duties without prior written consent of the other party.

IN WITNESS WHEREOF, the parties hereto execute this Agreement on the day and year first above written.

EXHIBITOR   THE BEST SHOW EVER, INC.

_____   By: _____

FIGURE 4.1   Continued

The Importance of Exhibiting at a Trade Show

Various studies conducted in the mid-1990s by the Center for Exposition Industry Research (CEIR) leave no doubt as to the value to exhibitors of participating in trade shows. Here, in part, are some of the results:

- 46 percent of decision makers purchased products or services while at expositions.
- 79 percent of attendees used the information gained at expositions to help in the decisions about which products/services to purchase.
- Follow-up contact to close a sale of 1.4 is minimal to complete the sale. A sale of "1.4" means that the sale was completed after contacting the buyer four times. Without participation in a trade show, it may be necessary to contact a potential buyer five or six times.
- 50 percent of exposition attendees cite "product accessibility" as the major advantage of attending trade shows.
- 61 percent of decision makers attending expositions cited product accessibility as their number-one benefit of attending a trade show.
- 76 percent of corporate executives attended expositions on their own or as members of their company's exhibiting contingent to assess their competition.
- 83 percent of corporate decision makers use expositions to bring them up to date on the latest developments and trends in their industry.
- The average attendee spends 13 minutes at each of 26 exhibits during an 8-hour visit to an exposition. Being able to reach that many suppliers in such a short time span maximizes productivity.
- 82 percent of decision makers found the exposition framework to be the most effective method of meeting and discussing developments with suppliers in a concentrated amount of time.

1. Set Objectives

We talked briefly at the beginning of the chapter about the importance of setting objectives, but primarily as related to understanding the show audience. All exhibitors will have numerous other objectives, which will of course be dependent on the company's specific marketing needs; but as a foundation, they might include:

General Objective	*Specific Objective*
Develop a new territory.	Generate 350 leads from this trade show.
Increase sales by 10 percent.	Follow up qualified leads within one month; write orders for $500,000 within six months following the show.
Test-market new product.	Survey booth visitors and record answers to specific questions asked about the product.
Increase product awareness.	Survey attendees entering and leaving the booth; survey 800 attendees by mail and 100 by phone two weeks after show.
Expand media coverage.	Send press releases with product photos to four industry trade or other targeted publications three months prior to the show. Follow with phone calls to editors to try to get feature coverage. Distribute press kits at the show and set up interviews with at least three reporters during the show.

Exhibitors should look to gain these advantages from trade show participation:

- Better awareness of industry and product timing.
- The opportunity to work in a prequalified buying environment.
- The potential to target marketing.
- The chance to participate in a competitive selling environment.
- The opportunity to make lasting impressions on attendees and other exhibitors.

Note

A show's fee policies should be contained in the exposition rules and regulations or on the application form itself. If they're not, the exhibitor should ask for them in writing.

2. Determine the Budget

Once the objectives are set, the difficult task of determining a budget can begin. This is a very important step, because only by carefully tracking how much was spent in order to achieve the company's show objectives—that is, the return-on-investment—can the exhibitor determine the direction and actions for future shows and how to save costs or even where to spend more.

Space Fees

An important expense is, of course, booth space fees. There are no hard-and-fast rules for how show managers determine these fees. Many will charge per square foot; others may bracket space fees based on location or size of booths. At multilevel exhibits, rates may be based on the level of the booth location. At most shows, however, exhibitors can expect to pay a premium for corner, peninsula (end cap), and island booth spaces that give additional and/or preferential exposure/visibility.

Exhibit space fees usually include only the most basic items: the right to occupy the designated amount of space on the exhibit floor; back wall and side drape (usually in predefined show colors); standard booth sign indicating name, address, and booth number. Utilities, floor covering, furniture, and so on are considered additional costs to the exhibitor (see the lists later in this section).

Some shows may include items ranging from tabletop exhibit materials to turnkey booth systems. The venue of the show may also require additional materials. For example, exhibit hall floors are generally constructed of sealed concrete, which necessitate the laying of carpeting. Other determinants of additional materials may be local labor costs, length of setup period, and type of show.

The following lists itemize other general expense categories all exhibitors should expect to include when determining a trade show budget:

- Booth design and construction
- Freight transportation for booth construction materials and contents
- Drayage for booth and booth contents
- Labor: electrical, plumbing, and janitorial
- Security service
- Floral service
- Furniture rental
- Audiovisual equipment
- Telephone hookup
- Utilities: electricity, gas, water, compressed air
- Presenters, models, entertainers
- Hotel accommodations
- Air travel
- Specialty advertising
- Exhibit staff training

According to various studies conducted by CEIR, exhibitors should expect to commit approximately the following percentages of their budgets to these categories:

Exhibit space rental	24 percent
Exhibit construction	23 percent
Show services (GSCs)	22 percent
Transportation	13 percent
Refurbishing (Years of use cause wear and tear on the booth. Parts of the booth will need to be replaced or repaired.)	10 percent
Miscellaneous	4 percent
Specialty personnel	2 percent
Specialty advertising	2 percent

Did You Know?

A rule of thumb equation for arriving at a ballpark figure of the cost of exhibiting at a trade show is to take the amount spent on the exhibit space and
multiply it by 4.

3. Design System to Measure Performance and Return on Investment

Just as an exhibitor evaluates whether or not to exhibit at a show, they
must analyze the sales and costs associated with the show. But how
that is done is as varied as the product sold. If the exhibitor is selling
at a consumer show where the product is purchased only at that site,
then the return on investment calculation can be done at the close of
the show. Did the attendees buy enough product to make more
money for the company than the cost associated with exhibiting at the
show? If the answer to this question is yes, the show was a success.

If an exhibitor is at an industry show, then it may take longer to
calculate the profitability of the show, as leads can result in sales
over a twelve month period. This leaves less time for an exhibitor
to assess the success of the prior year's show as the next year's show
approaches. Many exhibitors dilute their presence at shows because
they do not follow up on leads in a timely manner, so the attendee
forgets or simply buys from the competition. This makes the show
look less profitable for the exhibitor on the surface. Successful
exhibitors will know if the show was successful within three months
by a sampling of orders taken. Some exhibitors set up booths to test

Did You Know?

An exhibitor may realize income from a show as long as 12 months after the
close of a show, particularly at an industry show, when there's no "cash-and-
carry" activity as at a consumer show.

products and evaluate the acceptance of one over the other for their own marketing research.

4. Plan Show Promotion

Ironically, even with the growing popularity of trade shows, many sales divisions of exhibitor companies don't understand the real sales and marketing potential that comes from participating in a trade show. Furthermore, too often, a company's sales and marketing departments work separately from the exhibitor sales staff, which often produces less than optimum results, not just in sales generated at the show, but in meeting all other objectives set by the exhibiting company.

The point is, a company as a whole must understand the potential and power of trade shows if it is to reap all the benefits possible from its participation. To that end, the trade show industry can help by directing efforts to better educate exhibitors as to what they can and should do to have a successful show.

At the very least, trade show participation should be part of a company's overall marketing strategy, and not be regarded as an isolated activity. That's not to say, however, that promotions and marketing programs should never be targeted specifically at trade shows, but the best-case scenario is when it is integrated with a company's total sales and marketing effort. This enables management to set companywide objectives, which all departments can work to achieve in a cohesive manner. They then can set strategies, budgets, and time lines, and assign responsibilities more accurately, which will make it possible to more accurately evaluate the show. This will reduce, if not eliminate, the "We thought the show was great, and the traffic was good, but we didn't sell anything" syndrome.

Did You Know?

A 10-year study of expositions conducted by the Center for Exposition Industry Research (CEIR) showed that up to 33 percent of attendees visited exhibitors who had done targeted preshow promotion.

Prior to the show, it is vitally important that the exhibitor's promotion efforts work in tandem with those of the exposition manager, as described in Chapter Three; otherwise, attendees will be disappointed by the obvious lack of coordination.

As mentioned earlier, exhibitors should receive a list of registered attendees four to five months in advance of the show so that they have ample time to merge this list with their current client list. Then four to eight weeks in advance of the show, exhibitors should send, at the very least, a postcard to those listed inviting them to stop by their booth. These postcards or other mailers might offer small gifts or the chance to win a prize, or VIP passes for important attendees or clients, but their primary purpose is to alert attendees that the exhibitors will have a booth at the show and to remind them to schedule time to stop by.

During the show, attendee promotion can extend beyond the exhibit space to billboards along the highway, audio announcements at the venue, or additional entertainment or parties hosted by the exhibitor off-site during the evening. These events can be dinners, receptions, or theater or sporting performances.

After the show, promotion should be contact with attendees to close the sale and make the show profitable.

5. Design the Exhibit

Before exhibitors can even begin to think about designing the company's exhibit booth, they should:

1. Review and fill out the application form.
2. Understand the exposition rules and regulations.
3. Understand fees and payment schedules.
4. Find out whether the exposition floor will be divided by product type or category, so as to determine where they want their booth placed.

Space Assignment

Exposition managers follow no one set of rules for assigning space to exhibitors. Some use a point system, which may be based on one or more of these factors:

- Number of years a company has exhibited
- Size of previous booth(s)
- Date of receipt of application
- Fee payments (with application? full or partial payment? late payment?)
- Association memberships
- Advertising

Before signing on the dotted line, exhibitors should examine the exposition rules and regulations or the application form to learn exactly how booth assignments are being made for the show. If that information is not included or is not clear, they should contact the exposition manager and ask for further details.

Booth Design

Most exposition managers are understandably very concerned with display sizes and designs, and the impact they will have on the look of the show as well as on the traffic flow, so they will set forth rules and regulations as part of the exhibitor contract. Exhibitors have little or no say as to the booth they are assigned. The exhibitor makes requests of specific booth locations when they view the floor plan to the exposition manager. However, the exposition manager designs the show floor to be exciting to the attendees so that they will flow to all parts of the floor; the exposition manager wants to place exciting or well known companies in important or prominent positions. Therefore, the exhibitor may not receive their requested booth.

The following represent six common exhibit design elements:

- *Standard booth.* One or more standard units in a straight line (remember the in-line booth category defined in Chapter Three?). Maximum height: 8 feet 3 inches. (See Figure 4.2.)
- *Perimeter wall booth.* A standard wall booth located on the outer perimeter wall of the exhibit floor. Maximum height: 12 feet. (See Figure 4.3.)
- *Peninsula booth.* Exhibit with one or more display levels in four or more standard units back to back with an aisle on three sides. Maximum height: 16 feet. (See Figure 4.4.)

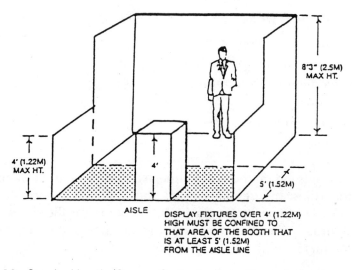

FIGURE 4.2 Standard booth. (Source: Center for Exposition Industry Research)

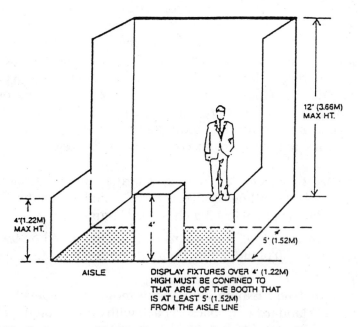

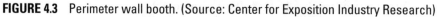

FIGURE 4.3 Perimeter wall booth. (Source: Center for Exposition Industry Research)

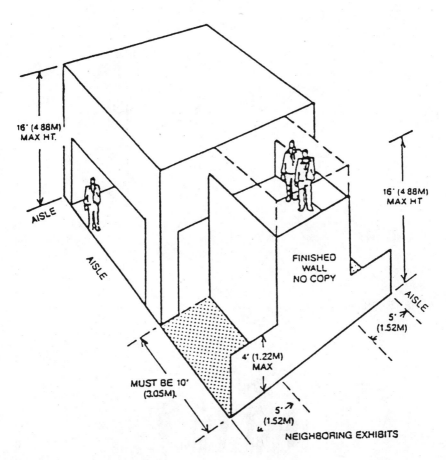

FIGURE 4.4 Peninsula booth. (Source: Center for Exposition Industry Research)

- *Island booth.* Exhibit with one or more display levels in four or more standard units with aisles on all four sides. Maximum height: 16 feet. (See Figure 4.5.)

- *Demonstration area.* Section of the exhibit space set up for inter-action of exhibit personnel and audience through presentations, product demonstrations, or sampling. This area must not inter-fere with any traffic aisle; and any sampling or demonstration tables must be placed a minimum of 2 feet from the aisle line. (See Figure 4.6.)

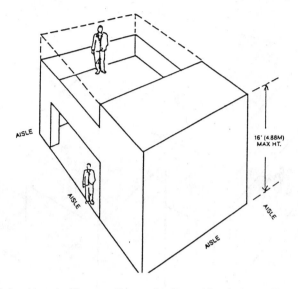

FIGURE 4.5   Island booth. (Source: Center for Exposition Industry Research)

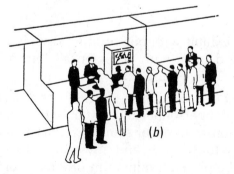

FIGURE 4.6   Demonstration area: (*a*) shows a correctly positioned booth; (*b*) shows an incorrectly positioned booth. (Source: Center for Exposition Industry Research)

- Towers. Freestanding exhibit components separate from the main exhibit and used for identification and display purposes only. Maximum height: 16 feet. (See Figure 4.7.)

During booth design, it is imperative that the exhibitor manager coordinate with his or her sales and marketing departments so that the vision of the company is apparent in the finished construct. It is also important to coordinate with the show manager, because some managers require that exhibitors submit—and have approved—their booth design plans prior to the show. Therefore, the responsibility of exhibit designers is twofold: They must create a booth that not only will meet the requirements of the show management, but, more important, be a display that will attract the attention of and be memorable to attendees,

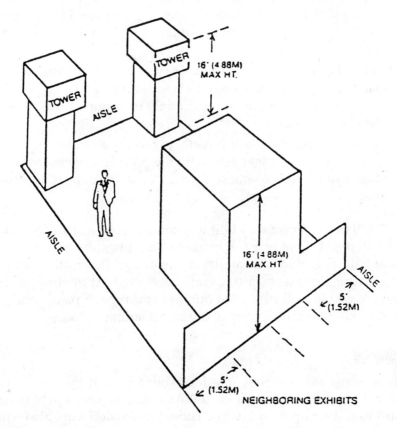

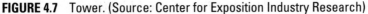

FIGURE 4.7 Tower. (Source: Center for Exposition Industry Research)

as well as comfortable for show staff to work in. This is not an easy undertaking. Exhibitors hire an *exhibitor appointed contractor* (EAC), to build, design, and install and dismantle their booths. The EAC may or may not do all of these tasks, but on the show floor they are appointed to do the installation and dismantling of the booths.

Shipping the Exhibit

Once the booth has been built, it has to be shipped to the venue. In general, one of these three types of shipment arrangements are made:

- *Advance shipments.* Made to the warehouse of the official drayage contractor or general services contractor in advance of the show. Advance shipments will usually be accepted at the warehouse as much as 30 days prior to the show date. Then the shipment will be delivered to the exposition venue at a cost per 100 pounds weight (CWT). CWT is how charges are calculated for the movement of crates, boxes, and containers by forklift on the show floor.

- *Direct shipments.* Scheduled to arrive at the venue, usually at the loading dock, and delivered to the exhibitor space at a per-CWT rate. Shipments can be made directly to venue up to one week ahead of the show.

- *Van line shipments.* Made directly to the venue and to the exhibit space by prior arrangements with the general services contractor. Shipments to the general services contractor can be 60 to 90 days ahead of the show.

A bill of lading (or way bill) will contain your instructions to the carrier that will deliver your materials to either the warehouse or exhibit hall. It should indicate the number and descriptions of each piece in your shipment (carton, crate, skid, etc.). At the time of shipment, the carrier will verify the number and type of pieces and provide the exhibitor with a copy of the bill of lading.

Setting Up

Once at show site, the first stop for exhibitors is at the service contractor desks set up to assist exhibitors with any needs they have in regard to setting up their booths. These service desks are also where all questions and complaints about labor should be directed—not to

Warning

In a union hall, exhibitors are not allowed to install or dismantle their own booth. The unions have jurisdiction over this. If an exhibitor does this work, the union has the right to charge the exhibitor anyway; or union workers may dismantle the setup done by the exhibitor and reinstall the booth, and charge the exhibitor for the dismantling and reassembly. Read more about unions in the upcoming sidebar.

the laborers directly. Most exhibitors will have placed orders for labor in advance through the *exhibit service manual*, commonly known as the "exhibitor kit," they receive months before the show, although requests for labor can be made on-site as well.

An exhibitor kit is a package of information sent to exhibitors from general service contractors so that the exhibitors may select GSCs and place orders with them. These kits usually contain options for furniture, carpeting, utility services, audio and visual equipment, signage, floral arrangements, and many more. The kits will also include time lines and prices.

Setup Schedules.   Many shows, especially those at which large or heavy equipment is displayed, will schedule the delivery of freight according to booth locations and/or booth size. This is called *targeting*, and it is done to facilitate a smoother installation and dismantling. Exhibitors must know whether the exposition is targeted, and when they are scheduled to be moved in. If an exhibitor misses the assigned target date/time, substantial penalties may be incurred and valuable setup time will be lost. Target times are usually indicated on the floor plan.

Did You Know?

Most shows put experienced floor managers throughout the exhibit hall to continually coordinate with exhibitors on behalf of the trade show manager.

Unions

Every city has labor laws with which exhibitors would be wise to familiarize themselves. Though there are some "right to work" states without labor unions, in most, the unions control who does what work in exposition venues, which can add substantially to the exhibitors' costs.

The following is a brief list of typical unions and their jurisdictions that exhibitors should know about:

- *Teamsters:* Handle all material coming into and going out of the exhibit hall, except machinery. (Note: Exhibitors are permitted to hand-carry small packages into the exhibit hall.) In some cities, this labor is performed by expo workers hired by the general service contractor.
- *Riggers:* Uncrate, unskid, position, and reskid machinery. Erect structured steel and other heavy construction materials. (Carpenters or millwrights may perform this labor in some areas.)
- *Carpenters:* Uncrate and recrate exhibits and display materials; install and dismantle exhibits, including cabinets, fixtures, shelving units, and furniture; lay floor tile or carpet; install and dismantle scaffolding and bleachers; "gang" chairs. In some cities, this work is performed by decorators.
- *Electricians:* Assemble, install, and dismantle anything that requires electricity to run. This includes, but is not limited to electrical signs, TV and VCR connections, audio equipment, and lighting. Extensive audiovisual setups may also require projectionists and stagehands in some locations.
- *Plumbers:* Assemble, install, and dismantle plumbing fixtures, gas lines, tanks, and vents that distribute air, water, and waste.

The following list cites the average 1998 U.S. labor rates (per hour straight time unless otherwise specified), according to the eighteenth Annual Survey of Labor Rates, published by *Tradeshow Week*, June 29, 1998:

Service	Cost
General Decorator	$ 46.44
General Drayage	$ 46.58
Carpenter	$ 45.53
Rigger	$ 49.08
Electrician	$ 46.85
Plumber	$ 48.63
A-V Labor (flat rate for delivery, setup, pickup)	$ 40.12
Forklift (lowest weights)	$ 80.16
Forklift (highest weights)	$117.31
Drayage (direct to warehouse, per CWT)	$ 40.49
Drayage (direct to exhibit hall, per CWT)	$ 37.43
Drayage (uncrated goods to exhibit hall, per CWT)	$ 50.16
Security guard (unarmed)	$ 15.04
Booth vacuuming (per square foot per day)	$ 00.19

Official show setup and dismantling schedules, as well as any restrictions in their regard, should be included in either the exhibitor kit or with the exposition rules and regulations.

Exhibit installation will usually begin with the larger, free-form island booths delivered via direct van line shipments. This is done primarily for logistics; it's simply easier and more time-efficient to have more space available to maneuver the cumbersome and complex exhibits in first. Conversely, there generally are areas designated on the floor plan as "late setup" or "freight aisle." In these areas, setup may not begin until a day or two before the show opens. And for those exhibits located in front of freight doors, setup may be delayed until the afternoon of the day before the show opens. Generally, these areas are for smaller exhibits that do not require extensive setup. Exhibitors should keep these considerations in mind when selecting/requesting booth space.

All installation and dismantling scheduling should be coordinated with the various unions involved. This can be done through the general services contractor; even in a union hall, the GSC will be under contract to the exposition manager to organize the setup and dismantling of the show. All labor is billed *portal to portal*, that is, from the time workers sign in at the service desk until they sign out.

While in the booth, supervision of labor is the responsibility of the exhibitor manager—even if a foreman from the GSC is assigned to the booth.

Dismantling. Dismantling of the booth typically happens in the same order as installation. Labor must be prearranged, and electrical and all other utilities must be disconnected by the venue or GSC-authorized staff. Then the shipping crates will be brought in and repacked, after which an *outbound bill of lading* is made and sent to the shipping company.

Did You Know?

When union laborers are in the booth as scheduled—whether they are working or not—they will be paid for their time there. The exhibitor is charged even when there is no work for them to do.

6. Train Show Team

Attendees in most cases come in contact only with the exhibit staff at a show. They do not see the expo manager, the venue manager, the general service contractors, nor representatives of the convention and visitors bureaus. The point is, their impression of the exhibitors' companies is based entirely on their interaction with these people, so if exhibitor staff have not been trained, or trained insufficiently, or are overworked, they may not treat the attendee as well as they should. This could spell disaster for a company, no matter how much preplanning was done and how much care and money was spent preparing the exhibit.

If companies want to reap the full benefits of participation at a trade show, booth staff should be:

- Well versed in their company's long-range goals and objectives for the show. They should also be given either hourly or daily goals to keep them challenged and enthusiastic.
- Trained to ask the right questions to be able to quickly help each attendee entering the booth.
- Scheduled into shifts so that they don't become overtired and overworked.
- Scheduled based on the size of the booth, to prevent overcrowding, and hence, inefficiency. A good rule of thumb is, two people in a 10 by 10 booth; in larger booths, use a multiplier of 2.5 per 10 by 10 space.

Finally, companies might want to consider some sort of special compensation for staff who "work the booth," particularly if the show turns out to be successful.

Conclusion

Once the attendees have all gone home and the booth and its contents have been repacked and shipped, exhibitors may be tempted to just collapse—justifiably. But there is important follow-up work to be done. Exhibitors should not leave without the exposition manager-supplied list of names of attendees. This is all important for continuing their sales campaigns. This list will include the types and numbers of attendees, and indicate whether overall attendance made the show worthwhile.

Back at home, exhibitors can use the list to assign to sales regions or to identify specific products that should be followed up on. The investment in the show should ultimately prove to be a source of financial benefit, enabling an exhibitor company to sell more product or better service, and to develop new or cement established relationships with clients.

ABC Trade Shows
EXHIBITOR

CHAPTER **5**

Venue Managers and Staff

The exposition venue is the site chosen to host a show. It could be a convention center, a hotel ballroom, county fairgrounds, a civic center, a park, a parking lot, a shopping mall, a football field—anyplace exhibitors have contracted to set up booths to sell goods and/or services to attendees. Yes, even flea markets can be considered venues. But for the purposes of this book, the term venue will be used to refer to convention centers built primarily as sites for trade and consumer shows and financed with public funds. As an example throughout this chapter, we'll be looking at the Georgia Dome in Atlanta, Georgia, a popular venue for trade shows (see Figure 5.1).

The growth in the exposition industry in recent years has created the demand for more such show space, triggering development of venues commonly grouped under the umbrella term "convention center." In 1996, according to the Center for Exhibition Industry Research (CEIR), there was approximately 63.4 million square feet of

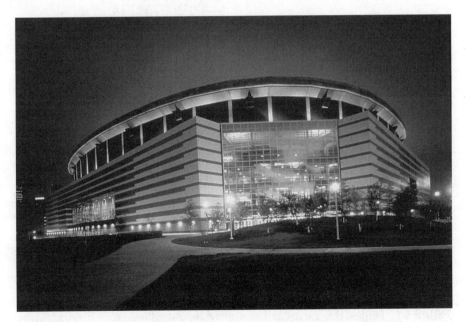

FIGURE 5.1 The Georgia Dome. (Source: Georgia World Congress Center)

usable exhibit space available in convention center facilities in the United States and Canada; a total of 448 million square feet of space was utilized for 4,400 expositions that year. Figure 5.2 lists the largest U.S. exhibit facilities, juxtaposed against hotel show facilities, formerly the most popular venues for trade/consumer shows. Figure 5.3 makes the direct total square footage comparison between these two venue types.

The venue manager's job is to generate revenue for his or her venue by convincing exposition managers to hold their shows there.

Largest Convention Center Exhibit Halls	Largest Hotel Exhibit Halls
1. McCormick Place, Chicago, 2.2 MIL sq. ft.	1. Opryland Hotel Convention Center, Nashville, 600,000 sq. ft.
2. International Exposition (I-X) Center, Cleveland, 1,765,000 sq. ft.	2. Concord Resort Hotel, Kiamesha Lake, NY, 177,347 sq. ft.
3. Las Vegas Convention Center, 1.3 MIL sq. ft.	3. Las Vegas Hilton Hotel, 171,730 sq. ft.
4. Georgia World Congress Center, Atlanta, 1,180,000 sq. ft.	4. Marriott's Orlando World Center, 150,000 sq. ft.
5. Astrodome U*S*A (includes Astrohall, Astroarena, Astrodome), Houston, 1,130,000 sq. ft.	5. Radisson Centre/Radisson Mart Plaza Hotel Complex, Miami, 148,000 sq. ft.
6. Kentucky Exposition Center, Louisville, 1,068,050 sq. ft.	6. Reno Hilton, 140,000 sq. ft.
7. Sands Expo & Convention Center, Las Vegas, 1,006,396 sq. ft.	7. Hyatt Regency Chicago Convention & Exposition Center/Wacker Hall, 133,556 sq. ft.
8. Orange County Convention Center, Orlando, 950,600 sq. ft.	8. MGM Grand Hotel & Theme Park, Las Vegas, 125,000 sq. ft.
9. Jacob K. Javits Convention Center of New York, 900,000 sq. ft.	9. Town & Country Resort & Convention Center, San Diego, 121,500 sq. ft.
10. Dallas Convention Center, 850,000 sq. ft.	10. Caesar's Palace, Las Vegas, 120,000 sq. ft. (tie)
	11. Chicago Hilton & Towers, 120,000 sq. ft. (tie)

FIGURE 5.2 Largest U.S. exhibit and hotel show facilities. (Source: © 1999 by *Tradeshow Week*®, Los Angeles, CA (323) 965-5335. Reprinted with permission.)

How Hotel Exhibit Halls Compare in Amount of Exhibit Space to Convention Centers (in Sq. Ft.)

	Average Prime Space	Average Total Space	Total Space Available	Prime Space Available
U.S. Hotels	55,884	92,980	6,508,600	3,841,848
U.S. Convention Centers	163,692	193,281	49,093,300	41,577,736

The average hotel exhibit hall offers about one-third the amount of prime exhibit space as the average convention center.

- -

How Hotels Compare in Meeting Space to Convention Centers (in Sq. Ft.)

	Total Meeting Space	Average Meeting Space
U.S. Hotels	8.9 MIL	129,738
U.S. Convention Centers	5.4 MIL	24,448

The average hotel features over five times the square footage of meeting space as the average convention center.

FIGURE 5.3 Comparing square footage between exhibit and hotel facilities. (Source: © 1999 by *Tradeshow Week*®, Los Angeles, A (323) 965-5335. Reprinted with permission.)

This in turn generates revenue for the local economy in the form of spending in entertainment, ground transportation, food service, and other so-called hospitality industries. Ideally, a venue manager will book shows one after another to ensure a continuous stream of income. The venue manager's ultimate goal to have exposition managers, exhibitors, and general service contractors moving shows in and out with just enough time in between for the building's maintenance staff to clean and make repairs.

Venue Development

At the beginning of the boom in convention center construction, most were built in the heart of cities, near existing hotels or financial

Did You Know?

The National Association of Exhibitor Managers was formed in 1928 to address the growing exposition industry. At that time, hotel ballrooms were the most common venues for shows, but they had become inadequate and not flexible enough for the different types of exhibits that were becoming popular.

districts. Now, more frequently, many of these venues are being built in the suburbs. Suburban convention centers offer many pluses. They are generally located in what are perceived as low-crime areas; parking space is usually easier to come by; and the atmosphere in general is more relaxed. As these venues have moved out from the center of town, hotels, restaurants, and entertainment attractions have started building to keep pace and to take advantage of the new opportunities.

Why would a community want to have a convention center? Taxpayers who support the construction of these venues believe the sites will bring in large numbers of businesspeople and tourists to their community, and thus improve the overall economy. (See the sidebar, "The Multiplier Effect," for the controversy that can sometimes arise over the issue of whether to build a convention center venue in a community.) In fact, venues of this sort have become such popular sources of community income that most major U.S. cities and a large number of what are termed second- and third-tier cities have convention center venues. *Tradeshow Week*'s Convention Liaison Council Economic Impact Study conducted a study in 1995 that demonstrated: "With $82.82 billion in direct spending being generated by the meeting, convention, and exposition industries in 1993 there is very little other evidence a municipal leader needs to support a large convention center."

Who owns these huge venues? A surprising number of people are not sure of the answer to this seemingly simply question. Most venue construction, nearly 80 percent, is financed with public funds or taxes. In the United States, fewer than 50 centers are privately operated, and most of them are managed by a convention center or hospitality management company.

Amassing the huge amount of money necessary to build a new convention center is difficult to do any other way. Sports arenas, for example, today cost upward of $300 million; even expansions to

The Multiplier Effect

The multiplier effect is the theory that each dollar generated by trade/consumer show and convention attendees is circulated throughout the local economy each time it changes hands—from attendee to hotel reservation clerk to maid and so on. Thus, that single dollar has a ripple effect on the economy. The multiplier effect is often used as the justification for the construction and/or expansion of convention centers.

In "Debating the Value of the Multiplier Effect: Is It a Fair Index of a Convention Center's Worth? (*The New York Times Magazine*, October 29, 1997), columnist John Tierney disputed the multiplier effect: "A convention center is a scam on the local populace that's cleverly presented as a way to fleece out-of-towners. . . . Suppose the convention center is never built and the locals are never taxed to build it. The money they save ends up being spent in the community anyway. Doesn't the multiplier effect come into play in this instance as well? This magazine brings revenue into New York from advertisers around the world. Does that mean other New Yorkers should be taxed to build me an office?"

In rebuttal, Steve Morello, president of the New York Convention & Visitors Bureau, said, "Don't trouble yourself trying to debunk the multiplier effect. Direct spending by visitors to the city creates jobs and, ultimately, contributes to tax revenue."

Tierney misses the point, Morello contends. "He is challenging the multiplier effect because it's easier to do that than to address the real issue; that is, that it's not in the convention center's mandate or charter to break even or to operate at a profit. Tierney may think that Javits or other convention centers do not pay for themselves. The convention center is any economic engine that acts as a magnet for economic activity. Why quibble about the multiplier effect when the fact is that 25 million visitors to New York are projected to spend $11 billion here in 1995? Convention centers are proven locations for people to do business, and that means spending money. The relatively modest investment for advertising and marketing a city or convention center is a tiny investment for a big return. Direct spending is what should be considered, and that is what yields the revenue for cities to reinvest in many city services."

extant convention centers can cost more than $200 million (see Figure 5.4). Thus, the owners of most such venues is the government, whether city, county, or state agency.

Unfortunately for the exposition industry, few elected officials understand how to manage these huge showplaces or realize the assets and liabilities of having a convention center in their area. Consequently,

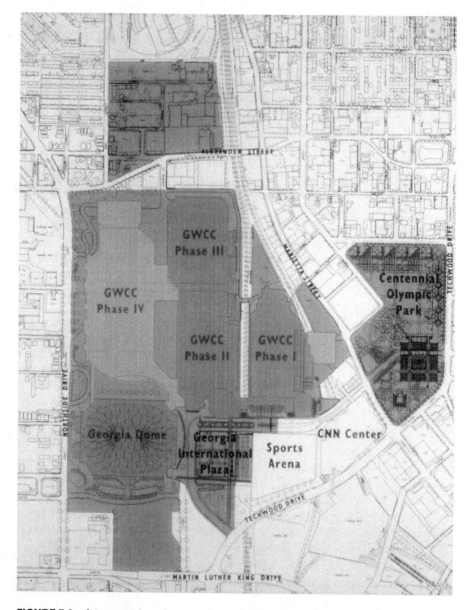

FIGURE 5.4   An expansion plan to enlarge the floor and meeting room space of the Georgia World Congress Center. (Source: Georgia World Congress Center)

it falls to the venue staff to educate the appropriate politicians in the business of venue management. To that end, many venues now dedicate staff to that task. Not only does this make the venue staff members' jobs easier, it also facilitates matters if it becomes necessary to expand the venue; government officials are much more likely to support a bill for, say, lodging taxation or rezoning if they understand the value of the venue to the community.

Selling the Venue

We discussed in Chapter Three how the exposition manager goes about choosing a venue. In concert, the venue management staff must understand this process, in order to be able to answer all the exposition manager's questions and concerns. One of the most important questions and concerns will always be how much *salable floor space* there is for the show as well as how the exhibit space is laid out. The venue manager will show the exposition manager a floor plan like that shown in Figures 5.5 and 5.6 of the East Exhibit Halls of the Georgia World Congress Center. The expo manager will evaluate the total amount of salable floor space in conjunction with other factors, such as proximity to the registration or admission area; see Figure 5.7, which shows the floor plan of the entrance to the Georgia World Congress Center.

Venue staff must be knowledgeable not just about their venue, but about their community as well. Venue staff must also keep their competition in mind when trying to sell their venue, and be prepared to explain how and why it is more appropriate for the show they're attempting to attract, whether they can offer a cheaper square footage

Did You Know?

All venues must comply with the Americans with Disabilities Act (ADA) to ensure that persons with disabilities are afforded the same opportunities to participate in activities at the venue. The legislation was designed to protect the civil rights of persons who have physical or mental disabilities.

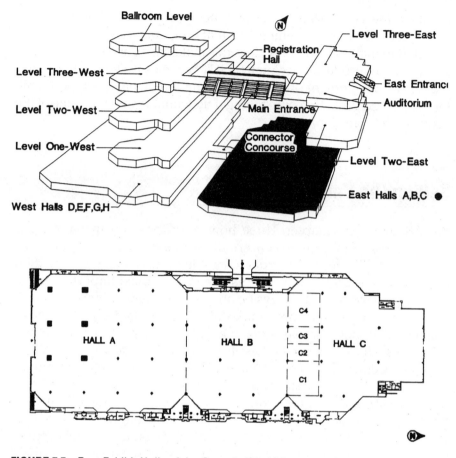

FIGURE 5.5 East Exhibit Halls of the Georgia World Congress Center.
(Source: Georgia World Congress Center)

rate, nonunion workers to reduce the price of labor, good weather, or a strong community focus on business. Let's look at two examples.

Las Vegas

When promoting a venue located in a gambling community, such as Las Vegas, venue management can cite numerous advantages: an abundance of hotel rooms, restaurants, and other entertainment options, as well as efficient transportation systems to and from airports, venues, hotels, restaurants, and attractions. Furthermore, because of the huge

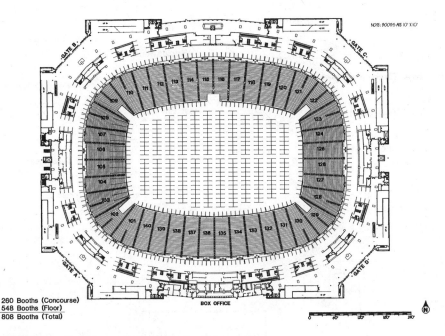

FIGURE 5.6 Exhibit space layout in the George Dome.
(Source: Georgia World Congress Center)

number of choices among hotels and restaurants, the venue can boast of lower rates for these services; in addition, flights to and from such places are numerous and therefore usually cheaper as well. Finally, such locales are well publicized, making it easier for show managers to entice both exhibitors and attendees.

The other side of the coin is, however, that a site such as Las Vegas may have so many attractions that it distracts attention from the show. Therefore, venue management must also be prepared to answer expo managers' concerns that such a site might draw attendees away from the show, thus preventing it from being as profitable as intended.

Chicago

Like Las Vegas, Chicago, too, is a popular "show" city. Venue managers can promote its many attributes, which include vast numbers of hotel rooms and quality attractions and restaurants, all easily reached via

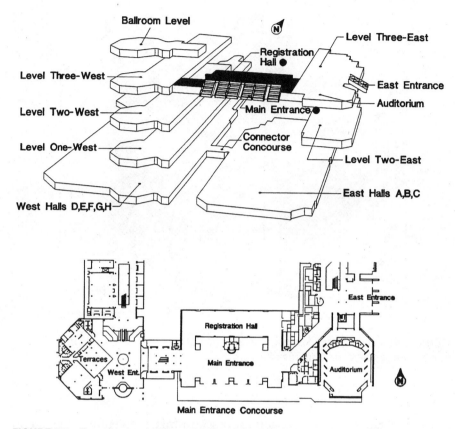

FIGURE 5.7 Entrance to the Georgia World Congress Center.
(Source: Georgia World Congress Center)

two airports and by widely accessible and numerous public transportation options. Chicago's most famous and largest show venue is McCormick Place with more than 2 million square feet of exhibit space.

On the other hand, venue managers in Chicago must contend with the city's big disadvantage: its notorious weather. It's not called the Windy City for nothing; and its bitterly cold winters and often hot sticky summers can detract visitors. Still, Chicago has had great vision for its venues, which continue to be popular show sites. But this is another concern of exposition managers that venue staff must be prepared to assuage: frequently, there are several shows going on at the same time in Chicago, potentially causing conflicts and inaccessibility to quality service.

We've been talking a lot about what venue managers and venue staff must do to promote and sell their convention centers. But just who are these managers? That's the next question we're going to answer.

Who Are Venue Managers?

Venue managers usually are either employed by the state, city, or county government that owns the venue, or for a management company paid by the owner of the venue to operate the venue. There are pros and cons inherent in both types of management system. When venue management is part of the government system, compensation—salary, benefits, and so on—may be based not on merit but on officially prescribed standards having nothing to do with the success of the venue. Needless to say, this can affect the staff's attitude and enthusiasm for increasing the value of the venue to the community. Worse, because venue operations and functions vary so dramatically from other governmental operations, the buying practices and incentives for the venue can be misinterpreted by other government offices, for example, fiscal services.

In contrast, when the staff is employed directly by the venue, they have a vested interest in its long-term success. Furthermore, venue company staff are usually more adequately trained to manage these sites and are better equipped to meet the challenges that arise and to keep abreast of changes in the exposition industry. However, venue company staff are generally not as focused on the venue as part of a wider community.

Venue management was addressed in the October 21, 1996, issue of *Tradeshow Week*. It reported that 70 percent of the nation's convention centers are publicly owned, and of those, private management firms operate 50 percent. Public agencies see good reasons to engage private management firms: to ensure more efficient operations, to increase the facility's income, and to assuage taxpayers who become understandably dissatisfied if their hard-earned tax dollars seem to be going to waste. Taxpayers generally see the private sector as more efficient and better able to improve the bottom line. Furthermore, a convention center is more easily privatized because it is not regarded as an essential service, like the police or fire departments.

Venue Management Staff

Venue management staff typically break down into several divisions, though there are of course variations from site to site. (See "The International Association of Assembly Managers" sidebar on page 104 to learn how venue managers have organized to improve their professional standing in the industry.) Those divisions are administration, sales and marketing, financial services, human resources, event coordination, engineering, setup, security, housekeeping.

Administration

The administration office is home to the general venue manager and his or her assistant general managers. The general manager determines the long-term vision and goals for the venue and its staff and sets the policies to achieve those ends. He or she also oversees all budgeting and funding sources, and handles the political ramifications if the venue is funded publicly. The general manager contracts with the exposition manager for use of the space (see Figure 5.8).The general manager supervises the staff, but will defer the decision making of most minor personnel matters to the assistant general managers. The general manager also coordinates with the local police, the taxi cab commissioner, and convention and visitor bureau staff.

In summary, it is the mandate of venue managers to:

- Increase revenue streams for the venue.
- Cut costs while maintaining a high level of service to customers.
- Generate new business.
- Understand the needs and concerns of the customers and staff.
- Retain and manage quality staff.
- Attract high-quality events and expositions.

The assistant general managers oversee the day-to-day operations of the venue, and coordinate the rest of the staff. They hold regular staff meetings and are present at all preconvention ("precon") meetings to verify not only that all aspects of the show under way are being addressed but that the current show coordinates with any other shows in the building or area and any other events in the area that might affect attendees' access to parking, accommodations, and the like.

Everywhere in the World Convention Center

License Agreement

Anywhere in the world, this agreement, by and between the Everywhere in the World Convention Center (the "venue") and the (customer) _____ whose address is _____.

WITNESSETH:

In consideration of the mutual agreements set forth in this Agreement:

A. *Grant of license.* The Venue hereby grants to the Customer, and Customer hereby accepts and agrees to exercise a license for access to the common areas of the Everywhere in the World Convention Center (hereinafter known as the "Center') made available to Customer and for use of the facilities in the Center, which are described in Paragraph A.3 (hereinafter referred to as "facilities").

A.1 *Purpose.* The license is granted, and Customer shall have access to the Center and shall use the facilities solely for the purpose of conducting the following event:

A.2 *License Period.* The license is granted for a period of _____ commencing at _____o'clock ____ m., on _____ 19 ___ , and terminating at _____o'clock ____ m., on _____ 19___ (hereinafter "License Period"). Within this License Period, a period from _____o'clock ____ m., on _____, 19 __ to _____o'clock, on _____, 19___ shall be designated and used for open show days for the conduct of permitted event. The period before and after open show days shall be used for the purposes of move-in and move-out, respectively.

A.3 *Facilities licensed and special provisions.*

Area_____ Use_____ Fee $_____

B. *Fees and charges.*

B.1 *License fee and other charges.* Customer agrees to pay to Center a fee for the grant of the license equal to the total of the sums set forth in paragraph A.3. In addition, Customer shall pay all additional fees and charges for any additional items ordered by Customer at the rates for such additional items prevailing at the time of the Customer's order.

Continues

FIGURE 5.8 Sample contract between the venue and the exposition manager, containing typical language of the legal consent and the responsibilities of each party to the contract.

B.2 *Payment of fees.* Of the total fee set forth in paragraph A.3 above, the sum of $_____ ("Advance Fee") is due on the signing of this Agreement. The advance fee will be credited against customer's liability under this Agreement. The balance shall become due and payable as follows:

_____.

B.3 *Rate schedule.* Center rate schedule applies to the Agreement and incorporated herein by reference, except to the extent the rate schedule is modified by the Agreement.

B.4 *Nonrefundable.* The advance fee and all amounts paid as partial payments by Customer are nonrefundable except as specifically provided in the Agreement.

C. *Insurance.* Customer shall provide to the Center a certificate of commercial general liability insurance, written on an occurrence basis, issued by an insurance company authorized to transact business in the State of Anywhere, including contractual liability coverage, naming Customer as insured and naming as additional insured (the state of venue and tort claim funds and other state-established facilities, the Center, and their respective officers and employees). The limits of such insurance shall be not less than $1,000,000 per person, $3,000,000 per occurrence. The policy shall provide that it shall not be canceled without thirty (30) days prior written notice to Center. The certificate of such insurance shall be delivered to Center not later than 45 days prior to the license period. If Customer fails to provide such certificate or fails to maintain the insurance in force, in addition to other remedies available to Center, Center may, but shall not be required to, secure such insurance on behalf of Customer. In that event, Customer shall reimburse Center for all costs of such insurance.

D. *Entire agreement.* This Agreement consists of the license agreement the Terms and Conditions of License of Agreement attached hereto, Rate Schedule, identified above. Any additional stipulations that modify, delete, or supplement the foregoing shall be set forth as addenda to the Agreement and signed by the Center and Customer.

IN WITNESS WHEREOF, the parties have signed this agreement or caused it to be signed by their representative, as of _____ 19 ___.

Center   Customer

Everywhere in the World Center   Any Show Management

By: _____   By: _____

FIGURE 5.8   Continued

Sales and Marketing

On the shoulders of sales and marketing falls the task of making initial contact with exposition managers, and thereafter, convincing these managers to hold shows in their venue. Sales and marketing staff must be able to address all exposition managers' questions and concerns about the venue and its location, and, ideally, develop a fruitful relationship with the show managers so that they become regular venue customers. It is more cost-effective for a venue to have repeat clientele than to have to attract new customers. Sales and marketing staff will use photographs of previous events to demonstrate the flexibility of their venue. Figure 5.9 shows a meeting room in use; Figure 5.10 depicts a banquet held at the venue; and Figure 5.11 shows the multiple levels of the exhibit space.

Once the contract is signed with the expo manager, an event coordinator staff (see below) is assigned to him or her, usually headed up by a director of marketing, who is aided by a director of sales or the

FIGURE 5.9 A meeting room in use. (Source: Georgia World Congress Center)

FIGURE 5.10 A venue banquet. (Source: Georgia World Congress Center)

like. A staff of salespeople will also be assigned specific clients, based on the region of the country or industry specifics.

Once an exposition manager submits show space requests, the director or directors coordinate with the assistant general managers to verify there are no date conflicts with other incoming or outgoing shows and to ensure that all space requests can be met.

Financial Services

This is the accounting department. They coordinate all financial matters—fees, service charges, and so on—with the exposition managers. They log payments from the exposition managers for exhibit space leasing and for any other service charges, including for utilities, catering, audiovisual equipment, and many others.

FIGURE 5.11   Multiple levels of exhibit space.
(Source: Georgia World Congress Center)

The accounting department also manages the financial well-being of the venue company; they write payroll checks and track purchasing, overhead expenses, office equipment, repairs to the building, and more.

Human Resources

As trade and consumer shows approach their opening dates, show staff always need temporary help, sometimes in large numbers. Immediately prior to and during a show, a venue may need to expand its staff by more than 1,000 employees for a four- or five-day period. And it is the human resources department that must meet this demand. Though similar in many ways to human resources offices in other businesses and organizations, the sudden expansion and contraction of the exposition workforce presents specific and difficult challenges for venue human resources staff.

Event Coordination

The event coordination staff faces some of the most complex and most important tasks of venue management. Without careful and precise organization and tracking, the myriad events, programs, procedures, and participants will not coordinate, spelling failure for the show. Event coordinators must work very closely with the expo manager throughout the entire year leading up to the show day, sometimes on a weekly basis. The event coordinator must know all of the needs and wants of the expo manager, and then meet them, while adhering to the rules and regulations of the building and understanding the exhibitor agreements.

The event coordinator must also know the details of the show's floor plan and schedule. Figure 5.12 illustrates various options for setups of banquets, classrooms, and theater spaces. The spaces must

FIGURE 5.12 Coordinating space usage. (Source: Georgia World Congress Center)

be laid out precisely to ensure the convenience and safety of the attendees. The event coordinator must also know how many loading docks will be used, what the temperature in the rooms should be at all times, along with hundreds of other details. He or she is likewise responsible for staying abreast of utility needs, cleaning requirements, meeting room scheduling, food deliveries, and more. In short, the event coordinator must be on top of every action and movement that takes place during the show.

Engineering

The engineering staff is responsible for the venue building, maintaining its structure inside and out so that it is safe and secure regardless of how many shows come in throughout the year. The engineers also determine when it is time to refurbish or to make repairs. This department also coordinates all utility needs for the exhibitors, to ensure that they have adequate utility usage, as well as to monitor usage so that no damage is inadvertently done to the building. In coordination with the general service contractor, the venue supplies electricity, gas and other utilities. In many cases, the venue staff will oversee or actually perform the duties of hanging signs and the like to protect the venue from being damaged by outside companies installing structures or signage that are too heavy or could somehow impair the venue building. The engineering staff posts notifications throughout the venue stating safe practices, such as how much attachments to the ceiling, walls, or floors of the halls can weigh.

Setup

As the title implies, the setup staff arranges the tables and chairs as needed, and sets up meeting rooms for show participants; for example, if an expo manager has scheduled a guest speaker, the setup staff arranges the room and the furniture in it according to the layout designated by the manager, whether in a circle, a U-shape, or around several tables (see Figure 5.13).

Note

The setup staff does not set up booths for exhibitors.

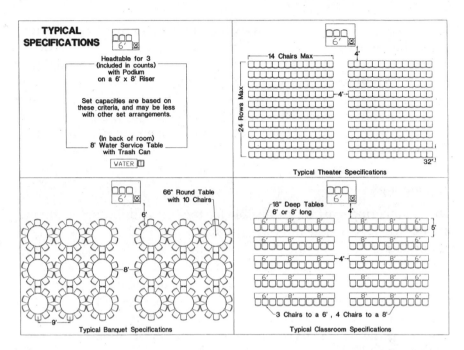

FIGURE 5.13   A meeting room setup. (Source: Georgia World Congress Center)

Security

Security has the daunting responsibility of ensuring the well-being of all the attendees, exhibitors, and other staff members while in the facility, along the venue perimeter, in the parking areas, and along the walkways; they also direct traffic if necessary, and aid anyone in distress.

Housekeeping

You could say this department does the dirty work. They clean the building, including all the public areas, the miles of carpet and windows, and numerous restrooms. They conduct maintenance cleaning during a show and do overall cleaning at the end of a show to ready the venue for its next guests.

Staff Meetings

With this diversified a staff, the only way to coordinate them is to hold meetings. Though time-consuming and not always as productive as they might be (as in any business or organization), meetings are a necessary evil to ensure that each and every event is properly planned. And because of the necessity for a venue to be booked as much as possible during a year, many of these meetings will occur two and three years before the event being discussed. This is to verify that nothing gets lost in the cracks, or that there are no scheduling conflicts. For tight turnarounds, when one show is moving out as another is moving in, all the venue staffs must be in synch. Naturally, various members of the team will also meet in smaller groups, such as the event coordinator with the expo manager or human resources with the event coordinators.

Venue Budgets

With such enormous structures and the staff it takes to maintain and run them, it should be no surprise that some of the major convention centers have break-even costs in the range of $45,000 to $55,000 per day. This translates into annual budgets in the $15 million to $25 million range.

Expenses

We've talked about many of the expenses incurred by a venue in the context of other sections, but here is a more complete list:

Staff: Includes benefits	Expansion
Maintenance	Legal fees
Insurance	Overhead
Special projects	Advertising and promotion
Equipment	Utilities
Sales	

Note

Security does not check badges or in any way monitor attendance.

The International Association of Assembly Managers

The International Association of Assembly Managers (IAAM) and its members are professional public assembly facility managers committed to promoting and developing the use of public assembly facilities and to standardizing practices and ethics of management and relationships with the public.

Active IAAM members include managers and senior executives from auditoriums, arenas, convention centers, exhibit halls, stadiums, performing arts theaters, and amphitheaters, whose facilities represent huge expenditures of public and private funds. These venues attract million of patrons to an astonishing variety of events from sports contests to rock concerts to conventions, conferences, and ballets . . . the list is almost endless.

IAAM also counts more than 400 allied companies among its members. These companies provide products and services used by venue managers. Through their IAAM membership, these allied members are able to present their products to this vast market.

History

The International Association of Assembly Managers (formerly Auditorium Managers) was founded on December 27, 1924 by six enthusiastic building managers with a vision of the future of public assembly facility management. Meeting for the first time in Cleveland, Ohio, their agenda was to discuss the important issues facing the auditorium management industry. From that meeting came the formation of the Auditorium Managers Association, later renamed the International Association of Assembly Managers. Now a worldwide organization, IAAM maintains the early commitment to the exposition industry.

IAAM membership has risen sharply in the past 20 years, paralleling a growing need for information, services, and programs. To serve these interests and needs, the association relies on the voluntary efforts of many committees to assist its staff and board of directors. As an adjunct to strong programs administered by the International Headquarters, seven districts provide a support structure and information network for members in each district, permitting managers in close geographical proximity to benefit from one another's experiences.

Mission

In December 1994, the International Association of Assembly Managers adopted a Statement of Mission and Objectives to guide the organization's activities. Its objectives are to:

- Promote and develop professional management of public assembly facilities.

- Foster use of these facilities for the benefit, recreation, and entertainment of the public.

- Cultivate acquaintance and communication among managers of such facilities.

- Circulate information of value to the members and the public so as to develop more frequent and efficient use of such facilities.

- Standardize practices and ethics of management and relationships with the public.

- Develop and maintain liaison with national and international organizations in allied fields.

- Provide such other related services that promote the advancement of the association.

The fundamental goal of IAAM is to contribute to the professional and personal development of public assembly facility manager members through promotion and development of quality programs and services. To that end, a number of excellent professional programs are held throughout the year. Many of these programs address broad management issues as well as facility-specific and "hot topic" seminars and programs. IAAM's seven districts hold meetings each year, offering opportunities to meet and confer with managers from the same geographical locations.

Publications and Services

The IAAM publishes the bimonthly *Facility Manager*, a magazine that addresses current issues facing public assembly facility managers; *Crowd Management*, a magazine that covers safety of patrons and problems that can arise in public facility assemblies; *IAAM News*, a semi-monthly newsletter that keeps members up to date on association and industry issues; the *Industry Profile Survey*, a series of comprehensive statistical profiles on all aspects of the public assembly facility industry; and the *Guide to Members and Services*, an annual membership directory and information resource.

IAAM also offers a wealth of services to its members, which include the Public Assembly Facility Management School, a two-year educational program designed for public assembly facility managers; the IAAM Resource Center, a clearinghouse for materials related to managing public assembly facilities; Online Database, a resource for news and information; IAAM "information packets"; and several training video tapes.

Income

We've talked, too, in preceding sections of how a venue makes its money, but to recap, income is earned primarily from leasing of floor space, meeting rooms, and other public areas. Floor space is usually charged on a per-square-foot basis. In large convention centers, this will run from $1.00 per square foot to $1.50 per square foot. The venue will also make money by charging for the use of the essential utilities—electricity, water, gas, and steam.

In most venues, the food and beverages department is a major source of income and a draw for repeat business if it performs above expectations. Additional venue income can come from parking, business centers for faxing, copying, and travel arrangements, and gift shops.

FIGURE 5.14   A multipurpose complex can be used for anything from a sporting event to a trade show. (Source: Georgia World Congress Center)

Conclusion

Today's convention centers offer extensive services to all the participants of trade/consumer shows, including food and beverage services, electrical and electronic communications hookups, water and sewer access, meeting and banquet rooms, and much more. In short, they are multipurpose facilities. They must be if they are to survive and prosper in this increasingly competitive industry. They must be able to configure into a variety of different "guises" in a short amount of time. It is not unusual for such a facility to handle in one evening a concert, a basketball game, and a trade show with no disruption to event managers, exhibitors, or attendees (see Figure 5.14). To meet that demand, newer large venues feature exhibit halls equipped with retractable risers and meeting rooms built with moveable walls; even the largest spaces have independent lighting controls, and are column-free so that floor plans can be changed quickly and without hindrance according to the design set forth by expo managers.

Being able to handle events simultaneously and/or in quick succession is the goal of these venues; it's where their profit is made. Multipurpose facilities are also ideal for exposition managers who need to draw and retain attendees. When attendees can go from meeting to show floor to banquet without ever leaving the building, it not only reduces costs for the expo manager, it also reduces stress and confusion and saves time for the attendees; consequently, they are more likely to stay for all show events, which is, after all, the goal of venue and exposition managers and exhibitors alike.

ABC Trade Shows
EXHIBITOR

CHAPTER **6**

Convention and Visitors Bureaus

A convention and visitors bureau (CVB) is, in most cases, a membership-based organization, funded primarily with membership dues. Members generally include businesses active in what is generically called the hospitality industry, which incorporates lodging facilities, restaurants, attractions, retail outlets, tour companies, caterers, ground transportation operators, and others. Professionals who may not directly benefit from the hospitality industry, such as accountants or attorneys, often elect to join a convention/visitors bureau to demonstrate their support for the bureau's purpose: to promote the community.

As the exposition industry has grown, so too has the role of the CVB, as pointed out in an article from *Tradeshow Week* (March 10, 1997) titled "New Demands from Communities that CVBs Demonstrate Their Value":

> *There was a time when CVBs were feel-good agencies. CVBs existed primarily to distribute information extolling the joys of visiting that community. That's no longer the case. Today's CVBs spend a large amount of their time demonstrating their effectiveness. Communities want return on their CVB investments.*
> *"Increasingly, our stakeholders in the various communities expect and demand proof of the economic return on their CVB investment. That can be a challenging expectation to fulfill," says Rick Binford, president and CEO, Metropolitan Detroit Convention and Visitors Bureau. All CVB's grapple with that.*

Traditionally, CVBs were primarily accountable for their activities; that is, how many people the bureau talked to, how much information was given away, and so on. Now a fundamental shift has occurred. The emphasis is on productivity, not on activity, says Binford.

Another major issue for CVBs is funding. According to Richard Green, vice president of sales, Greater Boston Convention & Visitors Bureau, "Funding issues are more prevalent than ever. Local governments have realized there is a lot of revenue available from bed taxes, but they don't want to share it with the bureaus." Green adds that it's difficult for the bureau to increase its members' dues because members

Note

It is the mandate of member-supported convention and visitors bureaus to represent all of its members fairly and equally. Therefore, bureau staff will not make specific recommendations to exposition or venue managers; instead, they provide the show managers with sufficient information so that they can make informed decisions based on their particular needs and requirements.

are spending money on such items as their own Web sites. Others are running at capacity and don't feel the need to market further.

Annually, the research department of a CVB will compile and report on its activities of the preceding year to its membership and community. If it is doing its job, this report will represent new dollars generated to the community's economy.

Relationship to the Exposition Industry

By the nature of its responsibility to market a community, visitors and convention bureaus form close working relationships with their convention center facilities. In many instances, the bureau will manage date assignments for the facilities, in which case, essentially, the bureau is put in charge of the venues' master calendars. Less commonly will bureaus be given the authority to commit the facilities for a given event; and with few exceptions, bureaus do not have operational control.

Many bureaus do, however, act as the marketing arm for the city's convention facilities, with responsibility for soliciting new business and coordinating services. (For an up-close look at one such bureau, check out the "Chicago Convention and Tourism Bureau" sidebar.)

Soliciting New Business

Exposition managers receive on a regular basis various forms of communication from numerous bureaus hoping to be chosen to host their events. In an effort to sell its city, convention and visitor bureau sales staff will send letters (see Figure 6.1) and other printed promotional materials, make telephone calls to explain how their destination can best accommodate an exposition manager's upcoming show, and place ads in trade magazines (see Figure 6.2). Bureau salespeople will

April 21, 1999

Ms. Shelease D. Smith
President/CEO
Elegant Affairs, Inc.
1358 Graymont Drive, SW
Atlanta, Georgia 30310

233 Peachtree Street NE
Suite 100
Atlanta, Georgia 30303
Tel: (404) 521-6600
Fax: (404) 584-6331
E-mail: acvb@atlanta.com
http://www.acvb.com

Dear Shelease:

Thank you for your reply card from the *Sales & Marketing* publication regarding Atlanta as a potential destination for a future meeting, convention, trade show or special event.

The Atlanta Convention & Visitors Bureau is prepared to help you find the right dates and space in our city or throughout the greater Atlanta region. From gold resorts in the North Georgia mountains to the larger convention hotels of downtown Atlanta, we are able to quickly check availability at a number of hotels and convention centers on your behalf. And of course all of our locator services, reference materials or promotional brochures are *free of any charges*.

I've enclosed our *Convention Sales Kit*. I hope you'll save it for future planning needs or, <u>if your interest is more immediate, please give me a call or email directly</u>.

Thanks again for thinking of Atlanta!

Sincerely,

David McAuley
National Sales Manager
Atlanta Convention
and Visitors Bureau
(404) 521-6394 (direct line)
(404) 584-6331 (fax)
<u>dmcauley@acvb.com</u>

DM/wfw

April 23, 1999

Mr. William P. Valusek, D.C.
Treasurer
American College of Chiropractic Orthopedists
1030 Broadway, Suite 101
El Centro, CA 92243-2379

233 Peachtree Street NE
Suite 100
Atlanta, Georgia 30303
Tel: (404) 521-6600
Fax: (404) 584-6331
E-mail: acvb@atlanta.com
http://www.acvb.com

Dear William:

I would like to take a moment and introduce myself as your account manager and to inform you of the services available through the Atlanta Convention and Visitors Bureau.

The Atlanta Convention and Visitors Bureau offers you help in not only locating the "perfect" place for your meetings, but also continues to support you with housing, registration, securing promotional items and numerous other services intended to make your job easier—and they're FREE! Atlanta is committed to superior hospitality service.

Enclosed is a small return information card which I would appreciate you taking a moment to complete and return. Accurate information is the initial key to a successfully planned meeting.

I look forward to working with you in planning future meetings, and if there is anything that I may do in order to ease your job, please do not hesitate to call on my direct line,
404-521-6623.

Sincerely,

Lillie McBurrows
Sales Manager, Small Meetings
404-521-6623 (Direct Line)
404-584-6331 (Fax Line)
lmcburrows@acvb.com

Enclosure

LMB/ltd

FIGURE 6.1 A CVB solicitation letter. (Source: Atlanta Convention and Visitor's Bureau)

Every city has a limit to how many

people they can successfully accommodate

at your company's meeting or convention.

Ours is about 3 million.

When it comes to hosting your company's big event, no city can offer you more than Atlanta. After all, we've just hosted one of the biggest events in the world. We have six major facility options that can meet your specific requirements. You'll be amazed by Atlanta's world-class array of restaurants, entertainment, shopping, sports, cultural activities, sights and history. And Atlanta has one more specialty that other cities don't - an abundance of pure southern hospitality.

AmericasMart Atlanta: Located downtown and just steps away from the hotel community, fine dining and great night life.

	Merchandise Mart	Gift Mart	Apparel Mart
Meeting Rooms..	21	4	1
Exhibit Hall......	96,000 sq. ft.	N/A	200,000 sq. ft.
Hotel Rooms.....	12,000	12,000	12,000
Theatre............	390	364	830
Ballroom...........	500 reception	500 reception	5,000 reception
	240 banquet	250 banquet	750 banquet

The Georgia International Convention Center: Just two miles from Hartsfield International Airport and convenient to the best of downtown Atlanta.

Meeting Rooms......	35
Exhibit Hall..........	112,000 sq. ft.
Hotel Rooms..........	10,000
Theatre.................	5,000 (largest meeting room)
Ballroom..............	600 reception 300 banquet (jr.)
	4,000 reception 3,000 banquet

The Cobb Galleria Centre: Located ten minutes northwest of downtown Atlanta; connected to both a hotel and specialty mall.

Meeting Rooms.....	24
Exhibit Hall..........	108,000 sq. ft.
Hotel Rooms........	5,000 - (within 2 miles)
Theatre...............	3,000 (largest meeting room)
Ballroom.............	4,000 reception 1,920 banquet

The Gwinnett Civic and Cultural Center: Northeast Atlanta's unique meeting facility featuring a range of facilities within a resort setting.

Meeting Rooms.....	14
Exhibit Hall.........	50,000 sq. ft.
Hotel Rooms........	7,500 (within 3 miles)
Theatre...............	4,000 (exhibit hall),
	700 (largest meeting room)
Ballroom.............	700 reception 500 banquet

FIGURE 6.2   Trade magazine ad promoting venues.(Source: Atlanta Convention and Visitor's Bureau)

Georgia Dome: Located in the heart of the downtown action, it's the South's magnificent showplace.

Georgia Dome

GEORGIA
DOME ®

Meeting Rooms	5
Exhibit Hall	102,000 sq. ft.
Hotel Rooms	12,000 (downtown)
Theatre	71,500 Full House
	40,000 Half House
	12,000 Reception
	5,000 Banquet

Call the Atlanta Convention and Visitors Bureau today and find out how we can help make your company's meeting or conference a huge success. You'll see why taking care of big events is not just a game to us.

Atlanta Convention and Visitors Bureau.
(404) 521-6619
http://www.acvb.com   E-mail: acvb@atlanta.com

The Georgia World Congress Center: Atlanta's world class convention center is adjacent to the Georgia Dome and within walking distance of CNN Center.

Georgia World
Congress Center

GEORGIA
WORLD
CONGRESS
CENTER ®

Meeting Rooms	76
Exhibit Halls	950,000 sq. ft.
Hotel Rooms	12,000 - Downtown
Theatre	16,000 (exhibit hall)
Ballroom	3,000 reception
	2,600 banquet

ATLANTA
Convention & Visitors Bureau

FIGURE 6.2   Continued

also makes calls in person to more formally introduce their community and its exhibition facilities.

Bureaus are frequently allied with convention industry organizations, participating in meetings and trade shows directed to organization executives and meeting planners. Through these efforts, bureau representatives work to familiarize executives and planners with all that their locations have to offer. Should an organization request, a bureau will send a representative to a board meeting, site selection meeting, or other related gathering to further acquaint decision makers with the city's salient features and services. And the size of the meeting is not usually a factor. Most bureaus are eager to attract business to its location, whether the potential client's need is for 50 guest rooms in a moderately priced motel or 5,000 rooms in first-class hotels throughout the city.

The CVB is the expo manager's central information source for advice on site selection, scheduling, transportation, entertainment, and other local services, usually at no cost or obligation to the meeting planner. The well-run bureau is equipped to provide current information on the city and surrounding area, as well as future planned developments.

Naturally, one of the most pertinent pieces of information an expo manager must have before making a site selection is whether the location under consideration is capable of accommodating his or her show's requirements. Are the preferred dates open? Is the facility available for the entire period, including move-in and move-out periods? Are all or only some exhibit facilities booked? Is there a sufficient inventory of both sleeping rooms and meeting rooms? A negative answer to any one of these questions could eliminate a location from further review. So rather than expending the time and energy necessary to gather the required information from several sources, the exposition manager goes to convention and visitors bureau.

Operations

How a CVB operates depends upon the size of the city it represents, which in turn dictates the size of its staff and budget. But most bureaus have at least one, and many have more than five, convention sales managers whose primary responsibility it is to promote the city as a venue for conventions, meetings, and trade/consumer shows. These sales managers may have as their "territory" state or national organizations; others may be assigned by organization type, such as medical, fraternal, or corporate.

Most bureaus operate on a lead system, whereby the meeting planner details his or her meeting specifications, after which the sales manager disseminates that information to all facilities that might be able to accommodate these requirements, to give them all an equal opportunity. If, however, an exposition manager makes a request for, say, a specific hotel, the CVB sales manager will make every effort to accommodate the request. The CVB sales manager submits lead form requests to the appropriate properties. The properties then send the exposition manager all necessary facts and figures to facilitate his or her decision-making process.

Services

One of the most important functions of any convention and visitors bureau is to service an exposition as completely as possible. Although the types of service offered may vary among CVBs, based on size and location, a number are fairly standard throughout the convention industry. Standard services consist of locating companies within the city and within the membership of the convention and visitor's bureau that provide:

- Registrations and badging
- City tour for families of the attendees
- Other venues for exhibitor and client entertainment
- Restaurant options for client entertainment

Most bureaus have a service department whose responsibility is to work directly with the exposition manager. The staff are assigned to assist the exposition manager with any problems or concerns with hotels, transportation, or any service that is provided in the city.

Chicago Convention and Tourism Bureau*

To give you some idea of how valuable the exposition industry is to one city, let's look more closely at Chicago's Convention and Tourism Bureau.*

As the official destination-marketing organization of Chicago, the CCTB's mission is "to enhance our city's economic growth by building a vibrant and highly effective team of bureau, government, industry, and civic leaders dedicated to maintaining existing and creating incremental convention, trade show, group, and tourist visitation through:

- Aggressive strategic sales and marketing efforts;
- Nurturing community awareness and alliances through greater cooperation with and understanding of all partners involved;
- Anticipating and addressing future challenges;
- Coordinating existing resources."

CCTB Membership

The CCTB has approximately 1600 members, in these categories:

Convention suppliers	30%
Restaurants	15%
Convention services	18%
Attractions/sightseeing	13%
Hotels	11%
Transportation	5%
Shopping	8%

Expenses

The CCTB's total expenses for 1998 were $7,203,727, accounted for as follows:

Marketing	25.02%	$1,802,445
Sales	53.94%	$3,885,495
Operations	21.04%	$1,515,787

The bureau's objective is to assist the exposition manager enough to encourage them to stay in the city for additional years or to come back to the city on a rotational basis with other cities.

Ground Transportation

One of the most important aspects of running a successful exposition is arranging for efficient and readily and easily accessible ground

Revenue

CCTB's total revenue for 1998 was $7,203,727, from these sources:

Membership fees	26.45%	$1,905,211
Grants	32.02%	$2,306,944
Hotel tax	13.88%	$1,000,000
MPEA grant	11.47%	$ 826,027
Fundraising	8.41%	$ 605,973
Other	3.30%	$ 238,055
Publication Royalties	2%	$ 105,000
Sponsorships	4.46%	$ 321,517
Housing	1%	$ 75,000

In 1998 (January through December), the CCTB boast these statistics for confirmed business:

Month	# of Events	Room Nights	Total Expenditures
January	68	146,442	$ 100,606,660
February	67	266,038	$ 327,314,250
March	79	242,145	$ 450,419,500
April	117	102,577	$ 74,852,280
May	103	107,944	$ 77,594,220
June	36	317,248	$ 379,194,956
July	66	149,558	$ 108,175,855
August	77	79,816	$ 99,033,600
September	78	153,658	$ 193,432,020
October	80	408,262	$ 616,828,778
November	62	310,443	$ 370,600,160
December	58	129,095	$ 227,707,210
TOTAL	891	2,413,166	$3,025,759,489

*Findings and activities from 1998, with a projection for 1999, cited in CCTB's 1998 Year in Review. (Source: Chicago Convention and Tourism Bureau)

transportation. Without reliable transport to and from the venue all day, every day of the show, exhibitors and attendees alike will become very frustrated and angry; and they will remember that frustration when they are considering next year's invitation to the same show at the same site.

The CVB's service representatives must be able to assure a potential client—that is, the expo manager—that all his or her ground transportation requirements can be met, whether in the form of private shuttles or buses, public transportation, or taxis. In most cases, expo managers will expect to make the reliability of ground transportation part of the venue negotiation. They will want specifics in these categories:

- Cost of services: minimum and maximum rates.
- Number and condition of vehicles in the case of private buses, shuttles, and vans.
- Availability: How frequently will service be offered to show participants?
- Reputation of private transportation companies. Expo managers will expect references and confirmation of same.
- Contracts. Will a portion of the transportation be subcontracted; if so, how will this be handled?

Conclusion

Convention and visitors bureaus are facing a challenging future. As hospitality businesspeople constantly reinvent their businesses to stay current and competitive to meet the growing demands of the exposition industry, the CVBs must find ways to stay relevant to their communities. Rick Antonson, president and CEO of Tourism Vancouver, the Greater Vancouver Convention & Visitors Bureau, says:

> We need to ensure that people don't take business travelers and tourism for granted. The value of taxes and revenue generated from these, as well as the jobs created, is apparent to us in the industry, but part of our job is to see that the CVBs' place in their communities is understood. Communities have a wider range of expectations from us, so we have to constantly demonstrate our value to them.
>
> Most CVBs will have to reinvent themselves over the next four to five years. Otherwise, we run the risk of technology or of our own members performing the functions we now provide, such as housing, information technology, and so on. We have to provide leading-edge technology so [that] meeting planners, trade show manager, and others look to CVBs first.

Another challenge facing CVBs is the increased competition, coming both from smaller cities and from cities abroad that are marketing their communities to exposition managers. "CVBs must define their unique marketing positions and sales positions and exploit that creatively," Detroit's CVB president Binford says. "Recently, some second-, third- and fourth-tier cities have tried to be everything to everybody," he adds. "Their marketing efforts point out that they too have shopping, convention centers, and other amenities that big cities have. Our challenge is to differentiate ourselves and to break through the clutter."

A third challenge is for CVBs to take advantage of the global growth in travel and tourism. "The world market is huge and growing," Binford points out. "Overseas visitors can be spending four to five times what a U.S. visitor does, so we have to tap into that market, but that's a challenge because we have limited resources."

A fourth challenge is learning to strike the right balance between marketing duties and community politics. "Stakeholders want us to be involved in political processes and public policy issues," says Binford. But that involvement draws on different skills from those traditionally required by CVB executives. "[CVBs] need stable and reliable sources of revenue to fund a competitive marketing program and to plan for multiyear marketing efforts. Maybe the time has come for CVBs to become a private corporation, since they already are expected to function like private entities." To avoid that, concludes Binford, "CVBs should be the focus of community economic development and must be the first stop for information and services for our customers."

ABC Trade Shows
EXHIBITOR

CHAPTER **7**

General Service Contractors

By now you know that the "players" in this group literally put the show together. They provide the manual labor and materials that bring the show to life. They transform the floor plans and drawings into the show, not unlike the way a construction crew builds a house from a set of blueprints.

As you can imagine, coordination and communication among the GSCs, the expo and venue managers, and exhibitors is imperative if the show is to open, run, and conclude efficiently and successfully. It is the GSCs' responsibility to "know the show"; that is, they must understand the exhibitors' industry; be fully conversant with the goals of the exposition manager; be familiar with the layout of the venue; and know and be able to meet the labor and scheduling requirements of all the show participants.

Background

In the early days of the trade show industry, there were no general service contractors per se, only "decorators," who made signs and hung bunting or draped tables. If exhibitors wanted to enhance their displays in any way, they had to supply any furniture, carpeting, signage, plants, and extras themselves.

As the industry evolved, so too did the roles of all the players in it, none more so than the decorators, who came to be called general service contractors, to encompass the wide range of services they provided. As demand grew, contractors expanded their service offerings to meet it.

What Is a General Service Contractor?

A GSC is any company (sole proprietorship, partnership, or corporation) engaged in the provision of materials and/or services normally required at trade shows, conventions, and sales meetings (see the ESCA sidebar for more information). Most are full-service general

The ESCA

Founded in 1970, the Exposition Service Contractor Association (ESCA) is a professional organization of firms engaged in the provision of material and/or services for trade shows, conventions, expositions, and sales meetings. ESCA is the voice of the exposition service industry or the general services contractors. It now has more than 100 member firms located throughout the United States and Canada. ESCA members vary from large general contractors with branch offices in many major U.S. cities to small specialty contractors serving a specific region of the country.

contractors designated by show management; they have sufficient equipment and staff to set up and service a minimum 200-booth trade show. There are also *specialty* contractors firms, which provide a single, specific service for trade shows; for example, provide and set up audiovisual equipment, wire booths for electrical hookups, do floral arrangements, and many others.

Today, there are around 100 general and specialty contractors. Two general service contractors, GES Exposition Services, in Las Vegas, NV, and The Freeman Co., in Dallas, TX, control almost 60 percent of the contracting market. The two companies have grown and have bought out or merged with other companies that were either very successful in their market or were very successful in a certain service. By merging with these smaller companies, both GES and Freeman have become stronger and more successful.

Doing It All

It is not overstating to say that the general service contractor's staff are the people who turn the exposition manager's vision for a show into reality. They take the show from paper to production. The general (as opposed to specialty) service contractor can do it all, essentially providing one-stop shopping for all the exposition manager's needs. This saves the exposition manager valuable time and effort because he or she doesn't have to contact and contract with numerous specialty firms and/or individuals and then have to coordinate schedules. One call to a general exposition contractor does the job. A qualified general service contractor is equipped to fill all exposition requirements and to carry out creative ideas. The GSC:

- Arranges for shipping, handling, and storing of products and exhibit materials.
- Handles freight deliveries, monitoring them from truck to loading docks to show floor and back onto the truck.
- Supplies labor to tape and lay out the floor plan.
- Supplies a full range of clean, functional, and decorative furniture and equipment, as well as carpets, drapery, special effects, and other display accessories.
- Installs and dismantles booths, including carrying out custom booth design and construction.
- Supplies labor to set up and move equipment, product booths, signage, furniture.
- Produces signs and banners according to exhibitor specifications.
- Provides safe and guaranteed access to vital services such as water, electricity, and gas. (Note: These services are installed by trained technicians in accordance with local regulations and codes.)
- Meets audio and visual needs.
- Arranges for graphics, floral arrangements, models, photographers.
- Posts show billing.
- And more!

As you can see from this list (which by no means is all-inclusive) whatever an exhibit requires, a general exposition contractor can provide or can arrange (subcontract) for first-rate, professional service to provide it.

Hiring a GSC

A GSC is contracted through a *Request for Proposal*, or RFP. The RFP is created by the exposition manager and contains detailed information about the show, including where the show is located, how many booths are needed, what type of show is taking place, and how many and what type of exhibitors will be attending. The exposition manager sends out RPFs to GCSs, asking them to submit a proposal and bid for their services at the show. The GSC is selected by show management, not by the exhibitors. The RFP must be filled out before the selection process can begin. The RFP enables a comparison among the companies, the GSCs, that are available for the expo manager's hire for the show. The following is the usual format of the RFP.

Definition of the Event

This is, essentially, the background section of the proposal. It:

1. Gives a brief history of the event: how many years it has been produced, typical attendance figures, average number of exhibitors, venue (if known) or of the last show.
2. Identifies general services contractor needs.
3. Explains goals of the show.
4. Lists financial options/arrangements that show management is willing to consider from the general services contractor; for example, payment prior to the show, at the end of the show, or upon invoice after the show. The same considerations are made for payment from exhibitors. Generally, payment from exhibitors is made prior to the show and when services are ordered on the show floor before exhibitors leave the show.

Requirements for the Proposal

This section of the RFP is filled out by the GSC. Information that must be provided includes:

1. A brief background of the company submitting the proposal.
2. Lists company representatives involved in the event.
3. Lists experience, namely other shows the company has produced, and where.
4. Explains how the GSC can meet the exposition manager's needs, and what qualifies it to do so.
5. Lists insurance requirements.

6. Identifies the approach—the game plan—for producing the event.
7. Suggests fees or compensation package.

After the GSC has received a copy of the RFP and returned it to the exposition manager for a final decision, the responses should also include the following:

- Experience: list of similar shows, either by size, industry, or venue.
- References: from show managers, exhibitors, or venues
- Company demographics: number of employees, number of shows currently under contract, mission statement, insurance coverage, payment procedures
- Sample show design: proposed floor plan for the show under negotiation
- Exhibitor kit design: details of what is included in a show kit, such as service order forms, telemarketing and online services
- Services: specifics of what will be handled by the company and what will be subcontracted
- Standard cost estimates: for pipe and drape, booth ID signs, pipe and drape for unsold floor space, aisle carpeting, aisle and directional signage, waste disposal, entrance units, show office equipment, standard furniture, custom furniture, registration and information booth setups, lounge furnishings, labor installation and dismantling costs
- Billing, order procedures: how orders will be taken and billed; invoicing and collection procedures; any discounting.

Once the RFP is complete, the expo manager can begin to compare among the GSC companies. Often, because GSC services are

Did You Know?

Both the exhibitor and the expo manager may be billed by the GSC for labor, equipment, and supplies.

Did You Know?

At repeat shows—those held annually or biannually, such as COMDEX—most exhibitors maintain their booth design and floor position from year to year. Not only is this easier and more cost-effective (no need to design a new booth every year), it's more effective for repeat clients, who will know where to look for companies with which they have ongoing relationships.

very similar, a manager will make his or her decision based on: a previous relationship or interaction with the companies, references, and reputation.

Once the expo manager has chosen the GSC, the RFP becomes the baseline for negotiations pertaining to the specifics of the show production, from considerations of the color schemes to the floor plan and delineation of responsibilities.

Getting to Work

The GSC's first consideration is the floor plan layout, understandably, since it's an integral part of any exposition manager's marketing goals. The plan must be tailored to make the most effective use of the venue space for both attendees and exhibitors, as defined by the expo manager. Together, the GSC and expo manager will examine the physical particulars of the venue, some of which will enhance and some of which will detract from the "paper" design of the show. In other words, what looks good on paper might not work in practice. Almost without exception, compromises will have to be made. Logically, in conjunction with examining the floor plan, the GSC and the expo manager will analyze the exhibitor attendee lists. Both the expo manager and the GSC of course want to lease as much floor space to exhibitors as possible, but they cannot lose sight of the fact that attendees must feel comfortable on the show floor, otherwise no matter how many exhibitors are present, the show could fail.

With that in mind, the expo manager and GSC will evaluate the types and number of exhibit booths, along with their content. They will need to know, for example, if a number of booths will feature entertainment. The floor plan will have to account for potential traffic jams, as attendees tend to congregate in- and outside of entertainment booths. The floor plan cannot allow visitors congregating around one booth to interfere with the business activities in adjacent booths.

With those considerations in mind, the GSC and the expo manager determine the types of exhibits that the participating companies will be bringing to the show floor. For example, exhibitors from the greeting card industry would obviously have less weighty and cumbersome booths than those promoting the automotive industry. Likewise, the greeting card industry booths would probably be more flexible as to placement on the floor.

The next step is make booth assignments, ensuring that attendees will want to see the entire show. Booths that attract the most attention, therefore, should be interspersed around the show floor to encourage attendee "travel."

After all of the contracts have been signed, the floor plan has been agreed on, and the booth assignments have been made, the GSC sends out exhibitor kits. This helps to prepare the exhibitors for the upcoming show; this in turn makes it easier for the GSC—well-prepared exhibitors are always easier to work with. Overall, such coordination efforts facilitate the move in and out of the venue.

Moving In

Moving in is a two- to three-day frenzy of activity. All of the booth materials and contents, plus the show decorations must be in place by showtime. Needless to say, it's a stressful time for exhibitors, GSCs, and expo managers alike, especially if they do not see the move happening the way they have scheduled or envisioned.

To ease this difficult process, the GSC will have coordinated, through its customer service department, these functions:

Did You Know?

Some exhibitors engage in a long-term contract with one GSC to handle their booths from one show to another in order to reduce cost and to facilitate coordination.

1. Shipping of all the crates and boxes to the warehouse the GSC has contracted for storage prior to showtime.

2. Arranging to transport these materials to the venue, using fork-lifts to move them from the loading dock to the booth space, and then assigning workers to unload the crates.

3. Constructing the booths, laying carpeting/flooring, and arranging utility hookups.

4. Removing the crates for storage to an adjacent area so that they can be easily accessed for the move out.

5. Placing sales products, hanging signage, and arranging brochures and other promotional materials.

This list only paints the broad strokes of a picture composed of hundreds of thousands of details that produce even an average size show.

Moving Out

Moving a show out takes place in a similar frenzy of activity but with much less stress, since there are no preshow-opening jitters. Furthermore, it goes much more quickly because there is less product and material to repack. The crates are reloaded with the booth components and forklifted to the trucks to be shipped back to the exhibitor's storage area or on to the next show.

Conclusion

Though it's stating the obvious, it's important to reiterate out how much labor and coordination is required to produce a trade or consumer show. Moreover, it's a never-ending process to find—and keep—qualified, reliable help, especially in the face of such strictures as labor unions, which require additional coordination of the GSC. In addition to offering innumerable services to its clients, a GSC must also be something of a politician, to be able to cope with and maneuver around the various venue and personnel obstacles.

ABC Trade Shows
EXHIBITOR

CHAPTER **8**

Attendees

To this point, the book has described the importance of four of the exposition industry players—exposition manager, exhibitors, venue managers and staff, and general-service contractors. Certainly, each of them is essential to the successful production of a trade or consumer show. But the true bottom line is drawn by the last player we'll discuss: the attendee. Though no one can say for sure whether a tree falling in the forest makes a sound, there is no doubt that if no attendees come to an exposition, there is no show.

Thus, most in the exposition business would agree that the attendee is, in a very real sense, the most powerful player in the exposition industry. When organizations choose to produce a trade show, their goal—indeed, their expectation—is that the attendees will consider their experience a valuable use of their time.

Two for Two

In Chapters One and Three, we talked at length about the two main types of expositions: trade and consumer. It should come as no surprise, then, that attendees are categorized in the same way.

Trade Show Attendees

The trade show attendee is marked by these characteristics:

- He or she is generally from out of town and is attending the show for business reasons.

- In most cases, the trade show attendee's expenses are paid by his or her company. (See Figure 8.1 for a list of the trade show attendee's costs for lodging, food, and transportation at the ten largest venues in North America.)

City	Per Diem Cost
1. Orlando	$140
2. Las Vegas	$147
3. Toronto	$155
4. Dallas	$168
5. Atlanta	$206
6. San Francisco	$232
7. Boston	$245
8. Washington, DC	$255
9. Chicago	$271
10. New York City	$305

FIGURE 8.1 Daily cost of lodging, food, and transportation in 1997 for trade show attendees at the ten leading trade show sites in North America. (Source: © 1999 by *Tradeshow Week* ®, Los Angeles, CA (323) 965-5335. Reprinted with permission.)

- Generally, the trade show attendee has an "assignment," that is, specific goals or objectives for coming to the show. It may be to just casually check out competition or products or it may be to gather detailed statistics; it could even be that he or she has been sent to be a "presence," to act as a representative of his or her company.
- A trade show attendee can't just show up; each is required to preregister, pay a fee in most cases, and, while at the show, wear an ID badge.

The trade show attendee has a business motivation, pure and simple. Consequently, promoting a trade show is done through direct mail to industry companies, organizations, and publications, or via corporate Web sites. These forms of promotion are very important to attendees; they use the information they receive to determine whether the show's content will make it worth their while to attend. If they perceive there will be nothing new at the show, they will spend their travel budgets elsewhere. In general, however, businesspeople place trade shows at the top of their list of sources of valuable industry-specific information. See Figure 8.2 for a breakdown of preferred trade information sources compiled by the Trade Show Bureau (TSB).

In addition, the TSB reported these industry statistics that further highlight the importance of trade shows to businesspeople:

- 86 percent of trade show attendees had significant buying influence.

- 83 percent of all visitors were interested in specific products or services.

- 59 percent were planning major purchases.

- Almost 50 percent visited at least one-third of those companies exhibiting in their industry segment.

- 29 percent (almost one-third) were corporate decision makers and check writers.

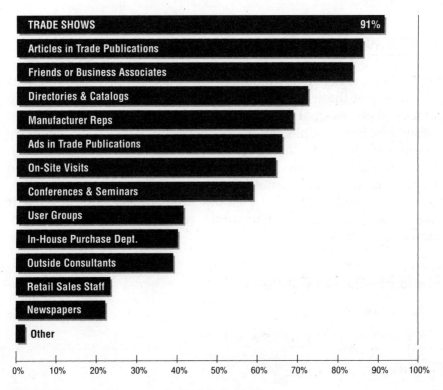

FIGURE 8.2 Trade shows top the list of information sources.
(Source: Center for Exhibition Research)

Consumer Show Attendees

In sharp contrast, the consumer show attendee has these characteristics:

- He or she is attending the show to be entertained.
- More purposefully, the consumer show attendee may be considering purchasing one of the products or services featured at the show, and so has come to comparison-shop, to get advice, and, ideally, from the point of view of the show manager and exhibitors, to buy.

From this description, it can be deduced that producers of consumer shows regard as their competition for attendance to be all other forms of entertainment: movies, sporting events, shopping at the mall, and so on.

Promotion Calendars

Expositions are held every month (sometimes every week) of the year somewhere in the world. These events are carefully orchestrated to coincide with seasonal product releases and the needs and wants of consumers. For example, gift marts are held in January and February for the next Christmas buying season. And, as we've discussed earlier, the production of a show, whether trade or consumer, is a year-round process. So, too, is the promotion process for those shows.

The following month-by-month breakdowns outline what it takes to reach and hopefully to attract, year after year, trade and consumer show attendees.

Trade Promotion Calendar

52 weeks

- Announce next year's show dates.

40 weeks

- Publish date of show in industry publications and on Web sites, and continue to do so until four weeks prior to the show.

21 weeks

- Launch first direct mail campaign.
- Begin exhibitor-focused campaign for attendee promotion.
- Design Web page to offer interactive registration, along with the opportunity to view new products.

15 weeks

- Send second direct mailing to attendees.

10 weeks

- Send final direct mailing.
- Launch second exhibitor campaign, and give out complimentary tickets.

6 weeks

- Conduct telemarketing for attendees based on preregistration demographics.

4 weeks

- Publish online show schedule.

2–3 weeks

- Distribute press releases to appropriate media outlets.

1 week

Hold press day.

Opening day

- Hold media reception; celebrate grand opening.
- Announce dates for next year's event.
- Direct video feed for online registrants who are unable to attend the show in person.

Consumer Promotion Calendar

20–24 weeks

- Establish online presence.

12–16 weeks

- Begin print publicity campaign, including sending press releases.
- Announce corporate sponsors.

8 weeks

- Conduct television/radio interviews with show promoters/entertainers.
- Target direct mail to consumers in specific geographic areas who are highly likely to attend the show.
- Launch corporate sponsor advertising, which continues until showtime.

4 weeks

- Place newspaper advertisements.
- Send press releases to every department of every newspaper.

2–3 weeks

- Launch television and electronic media campaign.

5 days

- Start directed newspaper and radio ads.

1 day

- Hold press day and media reception.

Opening day

- Celebrate grand opening, with public reception, ribbon cutting, and so on.

Days 2 and 3

- Direct media campaign to encourage walk-ins.

The Journey to the Show Floor

An attendee is an attendee long before he or she sets foot on the show floor. And his or her experience leading to the venue can impact his or her responses once on-site. The fictional "journey" described in this section will serve to demonstrate just how important it is that the five other players work in concert to ensure that a show's attendees make it a success. Notice in particular all the opportunities the hospitality industry (which, as you'll recall, falls under the auspices of the convention and visitors bureau, the CVB) has to influence (for better or worse) the attendee's first impression. Needless to say, if an attendee has a positive experience, he or she will be more likely to want to return to that city for another show.

Let's follow an attendee (we'll call him Tom) from the moment he gets off the plane and begins to wend his way to the show floor.

1. Tom's first interaction in the show city may be with a baggage claim person. Hopefully, his have not been lost. If they are, it's strike 1 against the venue city. But if Tom is given helpful, friendly assistance, and feels confident his bags will be delivered to his hotel in short order, it will be a minor annoyance.

2. Tom's next interaction will probably be with someone in transportation. Has the hotel or venue management arranged for a private shuttle for show attendees? Is it waiting for Tom when he walks outside? Or does he have to stand on the taxi line or figure out the public transportation system?

3. Tom's next exchange is with the front desk clerk at the hotel. Does he have to stand in a long line before he can check in? Is his room ready? Is someone waiting to carry his luggage and show him to his room?

Note

This journey to the show floor reflects the experience of trade show attendees, not consumer show attendees, who are, in most cases, venue-area residents. They drive or take public transportation from their homes or offices and usually do not stay overnight near the venue site.

4. Tom has now had a shower, and he has decided to make a quick stop at the restaurant on the corner for a bite to eat. Does he have to wait on a line there? Is the food well prepared and reasonably priced? How's the service? Was his sandwich delivered with a smile?

5. Now Tom's ready to head over to the venue. Again he must choose transportation. Has show management arranged timely shuttle service between his hotel and the venue? Or does he have to hop a cab?

6. Once at the convention center, Tom's ready to register. How long is that line? At some larger shows it can take over an hour to get through it. Not a good way to start.

7. Finally, with badge on lapel, Tom heads into the show floor. Are maps and programs handy and well designed? Is the show floor well laid out?

8. Now it's up to the exhibitors. Have the staff at the booths that Tom visits been well trained? Are there enough of them so he doesn't have to wait to have his questions answered or to be given a product demonstration?

9. Tom's been on the floor for about an hour. He's ready for a break, and maybe something to drink. Are lounges conveniently located? Are the chairs comfortable? Are there enough of them?

10. Three hours later, Tom decides he's had enough for the first day. He heads back to his hotel and asks the concierge for a restaurant recommendation for dinner. Does he or she ask good questions of Tom, to better determine the kind of place he might like? Does he or she offer more than one suggestion, with pricing options?

11. Back from dinner, Tom's worn out, so he heads straight to his room. Has the bed been turned down? Tom picks up the phone and requests a wake-up call for the next morning. Day one of the show is behind him.

This brief foray is meant to sketch some of the many factors that influence the attitude of the typical attendee toward the trade show. Though some of these factors will, of course, always be out of the control of the other five players, it should be obvious how integral each of their roles is to the success of an exposition, from the expo manager who makes the first call to the CVB to the general service contractor who laid out the floor plan to ensure Tom could find where he needed to go easily to the exhibitor who was ready, willing, and able to help Tom take care of business.

Conclusion

In a perfect show world, all five players in the exposition industry would always work together as a team to make the experience of the sixth player, the all-important attendee, a positive one. The bags would be at the baggage claim; transportation would be easily accessible and comfortable; the hotel staff would be welcoming and efficient; the restaurant wait staffs would be cheerful and timely; show registration would be quick and easy; the show floor would be laid out well; and the exhibitors would be exactly those the attendees were hoping to see.

Rarely, of course, does everything go right for any attendee. But when things go wrong, the other five players in the exposition industry should take on the challenge to make them right again. That is the true measure of a successfully managed exposition: when the players can rise above the obstacles and come out winners, both personally and financially.

ABC Trade Shows
EXHIBITOR

Appendix: Working in Exposition Management

The exposition industry, today more than ever, is a viable and growing employment marketplace in each of the six categories described in the chapters of this book. Identifying which of the six roles you're interested in and best suited to play, based on your personality and career goals, should be the first step in a job search.

You can begin your search by contacting local associations in your area in each of the six "player" categories. Also be sure to contact the venues and convention and visitors bureaus in your area and ask for a list of upcoming shows you might be able to attend, and names of companies you can get in touch with directly.

As on most career paths, the road to success often takes "travelers" first to educational institutions, and for those interested in becoming part of the exposition industry it is no different. Therefore, it is recommended that you also contact universities, colleges, and industry associations in your area to find out about course offerings and programs in trade show, event, or meeting management.

Currently, however, the Internet may prove to be the most reliable and rapid way to research the exposition industry, so to facilitate your investigations into this growing industry, the following list of Web addresses is provided. You can expand your online search using keywords such as: trade show, special event management, convention and visitor's bureau, travel and tourism, festivals, fairs, marketing strategies, and many more.

American Society of Association Executives (ASAE)

www.asaenet.org

ASAE is the largest society of association executives in the world. ASAE's web site provides a wealth of resources designed to enhance your professional performance, including that of the organizations you work for.

Association of Corporate Travel Executives (ACTE)

ww.acte.org

This is the only organization wholly dedicated to the science of business travel management with an international constituency.

Their website is designed to expedite research, solicit comments, and draw on the combined knowledge of the most accomplished business travel management professionals throughout the world.

Canadian Association of Exposition Managers (CAEM)

www.caem.ca

The Canadian Association of Exposition Managers (CAEM) is a national, not-for-profit association representing people who manage trade and consumer shows in Canada as well as people who supply products and services to trade and consumer show managers.

Center for Exhibition Industry Research (CEIR)

www.ceir.org

CEIR's mission is to be the advocate for promoting the value, benefits and growth of exhibitions as a primary component in an integrated marketing program through research, information and communication. They provide valuable marketing and research reports to thousands who have improved and grown their businesses.

Event Source

www.eventsource.com

EventSource is used by corporate and association professionals to plan conferences, meetings, training, tradeshows and sales and incentive programs. The site's BookIt! e-commerce service is a fast and easy way for users to research and book with more than 12,000 meeting hotels, convention centers, resorts, unique venues and suppliers.

EventWeb

www.eventweb.com

EventWeb is the home of the EventWeb Newsletter, which contains marketing strategies for meeting, conference and tradeshow producers.

Exhibit Designers & Producers Association (EDPA)

www.edpa.com

EDPA is committed to being the leading trade show marketing services association in the exhibit industry, by offering its members industry specific education, support, and services that will ultimately assist its members to more effectively support their customers. They serve organizations that provide exhibits and related services to the exhibitor in order to maximize their trade show marketing program.

Exhibitornet

www.exhibitornet.com

This site provides online resources for trade show and event marketing information. Visitors obtain late-breaking news, get tips on effective exhibiting, stay current with show changes, search the classifieds, find new products and discover new suppliers.

EXPOguide

www.expoguide.com

EXPOguide brings together exposition industry and Internet experts. Show and conference organizers can promote their event on this site. EXPOguide workers have the design and technical experience to put your brochures, registration forms, floor plans, seminar information, and other materials on-line, plus the exposition industry know-how to understand the critical needs of your business.

International Association of Exposition Management (IAEM)

www.iaem.org

IAEM represents show organizers and managers who conduct the largest trade shows and exhibitions in the world. A large portion of the IAEM membership consists of suppliers to shows, including full service general contractors, airlines, convention and visitors bureaus, convention and exhibition halls, hotels and florists—virtually all economic interests that become involved in some aspect of the show industry.

International Association of Assembly Managers (IAAM)

www.iaam.org

As a professional association, IAAM's mission is to provide leadership, to educate, to inform and to cultivate friendships among individuals involved in the management, operation and support of public assembly facilities. The site has, among other things, an interactive directory, a resource center with a listing of products and services for sale, and a magazine.

International Association of Conference Centers (IACC)

www.iacconline.com

This is a not-for-profit organization founded in 1981 to advance understanding and awareness of conference centers as distinct and unique within the hospitality industry. The site has a "Planners Only" section for the meeting professional to archive their Requests for Proposal and get industry news. Members can also network with other conference professionals and post press releases.

Knowledge Web

www.kweb.com

KnowledgeWeb, Inc. was founded in September, 1994 by David and Kelli Fox to create original content and digital commerce applications for the Internet, broadband networks, and connected consumer devices. The company has established a formidable distribution network including more than 250 content syndication and commerce affiliation partnerships.

Meeting Planners International (MPI)

www.mpiweb.org

Meeting Professionals International (MPI) is the world's largest association of meeting professionals with more than 17,000 members in 64 countries. The site has a calendar of industry events, a resource center with online bookstore, meeting resource directories, a Supplier Showcase, conference registration forms, and information on upcoming educational opportunities.

National Motorcoach Network

www.motorcoach.com

This site has a National Reservation Center that provides bus and charter/tour motorcoach equipment that meets the toughest safety and quality standards in the industry.

Professional Convention Management Association (PCMA)

www.pcma.org

This organization offers information about the meetings industry. Their site covers the following topics—research studies, job types, PCMA's Network for the Needy, PCMA membership information, PCMA products and services, North American Meetings Databank service, checklists, continuing education opportunities, student scholarship information and student activities.

The Trade Group

www.tradegroup.com

The Trade Group is a team of professionals in the business of using visual and structural impact to make your exhibit more engaging than all others by presenting information in an intriguing, involving and memorable way. The site has information on creative design, graphics, exhibits, corporate rental, storage and management, installation and dismantling, and rental packages.

Trade Show Exhibitors Association (TSEA)

www.tsea.org

This organization provides knowledge to marketing and management professionals who use exhibits to promote and sell their products, both domestically and abroad, as well as those who supply them with products and services. Their site has a trade show search engine, bookstore, an articles archive, and TSEA's online publications.

ABC Trade Shows EXHIBITOR

Index